The Ideal

Your Guide to An Ideal Life

The Ideal

Your Guide to An Ideal Life

(Monochrome Edition)

John H. Clark III

BFG PRESS
HONOLULU

Edited by The PIE Group
Published by BFG Press LLC
For information address:
BFG Press
P.O. Box 2269, Honolulu, HI 96706
www.BFGPRESS.com

ISBN 978-0-9820307-4-5
Printed in the United States of America
Library of Congress Control Number: 2011919434
2
Cover design and cover photo by Maritza Lopez Holland

Books are available in quantity for promotional/premium use.
Send inquiries to info@bfgpress.com.

Powerful Premises Published ®
is a registered trademark of BFG Press
All Rights Reserved

A full-color version of this book is available.
Please order ISBN 978-0-9820307-3-8

For Sophia and Gabriella

Table of Contents

Foreword

By Dr. A. Moorin

To truly appreciate the pearls of wisdom in *The Ideal*, you need to know the author himself.

John Clark is a man of action and accomplishment. A veteran, author, father, husband, and passionate personal coach for many successful people, he has created a legacy of enlightenment.

In this current volume, he takes the mystery out of self-improvement and sets aside the clichés of most self-help books. Revealing simple but practical truths, he demonstrates how readers can improve their lives by simply focusing on things that matter more than anything else: themselves.

In a simple, self-questioning, workbook format, he asks readers to examine themselves, their strengths, and their priorities to solve their problems, transform their situations, accomplish their goals, and lead happy, **fulfilling** lives.

Breaking down the title of *The Ideal* into its component letters with different but complementary meanings (I, Id, Idea, Deal, Ideal), he explains how each word part contributes to a person's self-knowledge.

Notice the word "deal" suggests that we are, in fact, making an agreement between our outer self and our inner self... and between our self and the world... to live our ideal lives.

Clark then deals with *The Ideal* world, its values, its obstacles, and the practical methods for overcoming those obstacles, and their potential results.

In perhaps the most powerful section, Clark explains how situations have multiple points of view – one's own point of view, someone else's point of view, and the Truth - all of which deserve scrutiny - before we can improve our perceptions and therefore our respective actions.

The Ideal is a short book but a worthwhile one.

As someone once said, "*Wisdom sometimes comes in small packages.*" *The Ideal* is proof of that truth.

Aristotle reminds us, "*Contemplation is the highest form of wisdom.*" Yet we must add that *knowledge without action is like a voyage without a ship.*

The Ideal provides the knowledge **and** the navigation tools so that you can say with William Henley in "Invictus,"

"I am the master of my fate...

...the captain of my soul."

Preface: *Not just any old idea*

Why did I write this book? Why is it titled "*The Ideal*"? And how will this book affect you?

Well, let me start by saying this: **Trust me, I'm going somewhere with this.**

Although the word god (with a little 'g') appears on pages 48 and 49, this is not a religious book. (Go ahead and flip to those pages now if you'd like). And this is not a book full of feel-good stories to make you feel good about life.

Trust me...

This is a book about **changing** your life!

Perhaps I am asking & tasking too much from you.

After all, *trust* is such an absolute ideal. *Trust* is such a fragile entity.

Trust is such an intimate portrait of a relationship. *Or is it?* Friends, family, strangers, and organizations often say, "*Trust me!*" And, for the most part, we are quite willing to give our valuable trust to other people and organizations.

The daycare center where parents park their children is asking quite a bit from those parents. It is overtly telling those parents, "*Trust me!*"

The billboard sign peddling food products or financial services screams, "*Trust me!*" People, products, and posters all say, "*Trust me!*"

But questions remain: Whom **can** you trust? Whom **do** you trust? Whom **will** you trust?

Trust me...

When I say, *"Trust me, I'm going somewhere with this,"* I am simply stating the obvious. I am clearly stating what is implied when newspapers publish articles, or when studios make television shows and movies. Likewise, every time elected officials speak publicly, they are asking for our trust.

And what do **we** do?

We trust the newspaper, the ad, and the television show. In fact, when we read a book, we allow the author to take us to a different vantage point; we allow the creator of that manuscript to escort our minds to a predetermined destination. But, *to where is the author taking you?* We have no idea!

Before I ask you to invest additional trust in this book, please keep in mind that, in many respects, you will be a changed person when you have finished reading *The Ideal.*

The world, though not significantly different than when you initially began reading *The Ideal,* will begin to appear different, simply because you will gain insight into a vastly different "reality."

In reality, here is how this book came to be:

As a young man born in Michigan, I was an avid runner during the summer, and I longed to see the world outside of the frosty fall and perennially white winters.

Later in life, amidst a career travelling abroad, I underwent two knee surgeries after sustaining an injury during military operations in Iraq.

Several years later, I achieved my childhood dream of owning a home in Hawaii. However, as an adult living in Hawaii, my knee injuries, though not particularly serious, prevented me from running. Alas, I could no longer run... but I *could* still walk. And as much as I had previously loved running, I soon developed a fond appreciation for walks early in the morning.

But the scope of my job responsibilities had grown overwhelmingly out of control. And with multiple offices in Hawaii and Guam, my career began to take more than a physical toll on my life. In fact, in just a few short months, I had allowed my career to consume every aspect of my life, including my family, social, and creative lives.

My house in Hawaii became a mere rest stop between meetings, travel, political posturing, strategic emails, emerging-policy implementation, and so many other "important" things.

I was working at least 80 hours every week; our three-year-old daughter wouldn't kiss Daddy; and my smartphone had become my alarm clock, my 24-hour tether, and my most trusted assistant.

Yet, amidst all the chaos, I refused to give up my morning walks. So to keep my stress levels manageable, and to thoroughly think through my daily thoughts, I eventually began scheduling hour-long walks at 4 o'clock in the morning. I would arise at 3:50 AM, and I made it my goal to be off the front porch no later than 4:15 AM.

At first glance, people might say such a strategy is insane. But for me, that golden hour of silence... that time of solitude and soul-searching proved to be the greatest gift I have ever given myself.

The question is: *Did I really give this gift to myself?* After all, it was the knee injury that caused me to seek an alternate path to running (pardon the pun). And it was my hellacious schedule that led me to the 4:00 AM walks. And it was during one of those early morning walks that I kept asking myself about *The Ideal life.*

The ideal life... what a novel concept!

And on one fateful morning, under a canopy of stars and light from billions of miles away, I was given the map to find a key to a world that can exist within the most demanding swirls of chaos.

On that fateful morning, my intuition repeatedly asked me to look deep into *The Ideal...*

... not just any old idea.

Over and over again, as I thoughtfully paced into the darkness and then returned to my family's front door, my intuition repeatedly asked me to dismantle the word "*ideal.*" And then it struck me. The word *ideal* is actually a conglomeration of several smaller words, specifically:

~ I ~ ID ~ IDEA ~ DEAL ~ IDEAL ~

"Wow!" I said to myself. *"This is unbelievable!"*

Then, there, and now, I will tell you what my intuition tells me to this very day...

Trust me: *This is the real **deal...***

~ John H. Clark, III ~

Part 1: Getting Started

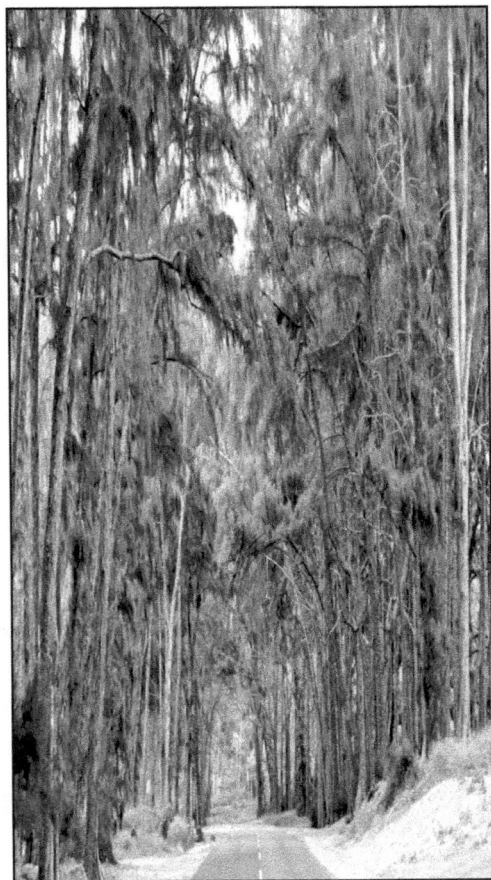

A stand can be made against

invasion by an army.

No stand can be made

against invasion by an **idea**.

~ *Victor Hugo*

Believing *is one thing...*

Knowing *is everything.*

~ *John H. Clark III*

Traditionally, when you read a book, all the great information is situated somewhere near the end of the book. *The Ideal* is not your traditional book.

Traditionally, when people read through a good book on real life, they tend to lull themselves into a soft sort of denial... reading through the pages as if the knowledge within the book applies only to he, she, and other people - and not to you or me.

Traditionally, people tend to think of life **improvements** as *self-help* and touchy feely.

This book is neither touchy feely nor self-help.

This is a straightforward, no-nonsense, practical & purposeful map on **HOW** to achieve an ideal life.

This is not your traditional book.

Up until now, your birthplace, your family culture, your childhood, and your previous life experiences have quite a bit to say about who you **are**.

On the other hand, all those things have little or nothing to say about who you can **become**.

From this point on, *The Ideal* concept of who you can become is based entirely upon whether or not you accept and adapt to the principles provided herein. If you can simply accept these simple-but-powerful principles, you **will** learn how to adapt to your most challenging situations. Best of all... when you accept and adapt to the principles herein, you **will** achieve *The Ideal* life. But first...

We must consider life itself.

This Thing Called Life

How do you define *life*?

Is life defined by what *has* happened?

Is life defined by what *will* happen?

Is life defined by what *is happening*?

Or is life defined by some other definition that you or someone else tracks daily?

In the truest sense, *life is **now***.

Indeed, as our lives have evolved, the individual weeks, months, and years have flowed one into the other, reaching heights of joy and falling deep into the depths of despair at one point or another.

That is life in the collective sense.

However, life in the collective sense tends to actually diminish life and the significance of today.

Life in the collective sense has a *propensity* to gloss over how significant today really is.

In the overall scheme of things, the last ten years may appear to be more important than today.

However, in reality, you absolutely, positively cannot change the last ten years...

And you cannot change the day that *is* yesterday.

On the other hand, today really is at your disposal.
Today is wrapped up and captured by
the power of you.

Today is all you really have.

So... How do you change your very own life?

How do you get to **There** from **here**?

Start with today.

Use today to change tomorrow.

More specifically: Today, you will use the roadmap
on the next 200 pages to change the next 20 days.

Today, your life changes forever.

The only difference between "*There*" and "*here*" is
the Capital 'T'... that is the Capital 'T' Truth.

Are you ready to face the Capital 'T' Truth of life?

If so, let's get ready to tackle your issues!

T

What is your current challenge in life?

What events are you grappling with right now?

By the time you finish this book, you will clearly understand how to move past *any* situation. Best of all, you will literally become more powerful, specifically *because of* those exact same situations.

Upon completing **The Ideal**, you will have a full-blown education on how to achieve **The Ideal** life.

The next few pages provide a quick and basic overview of the principles presented in this book. Initially, you may believe the principles are far too simple to have any sort of lasting, positive change.

At this point, your beliefs are not what matters.

What you *know*
is what really matters!

What is your name?

Do you *believe* it is your name?

...or do you *know* it?

Where do you live?

Do you **believe** where you live?

...or do you **know** where you live?

Why do you breathe?

Do you **believe** you need air to live?

...or do you **know** you need air?

The above questions may appear silly. As silly as it may seem, please consider a very important point before reading further into this little book: (To you) your beliefs matter more than the truth.

To truly understand the significant **Truths** discussed in the later chapters of this book, let's review some basic **Truths** about life.

For the most part, *believing* someone did this or that is far different than *knowing* someone did this or that. *Believing* something happened here or there... is far different than *knowing* something happened here or there. Accordingly, at this point, your beliefs don't really matter. However...

...what you **know** matters most of all.

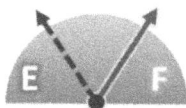

Think of your mind as a fuel tank for your life.

The picture above represents that fuel tank.

Looking at the picture, the dashed arrow on the left represents the **bad** ideas and all the negativity floating around in your conscious and subconscious thoughts. The solid arrow on the right represents all the **good** ideas and positivity floating around in your thoughts. Your head is the fuel tank where all your ideas live.

And your ideas are the things that drive your life.

When you fill your **mind** (your inner world) with (only) positive thoughts, your *life* (your outer world) will be fueled by those positive thoughts. When you fill your inner world with positive thoughts, your life will be fueled by the best thoughts, the best intentions, and the best actions.

To achieve an ideal life, your goal is to maximize the good things in life while minimizing the bad things. And since every single action starts with a thought, your goal is to start thinking only good thoughts.

Essentially, the previous paragraph is an overview of this book. But can **The Ideal** really be that simple? Yes. It is that simple. The question is...

"Is it really that **easy**?" Let's get started!

POSITIVE

Moving Forward...

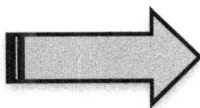

Without a beginning,
　　　　　...there is no end.

Without a beginning
　　　　and an end,
　　　　　there is no path.

Without a path,
　　　　there is no journey.

Without the journey,
　　　　there is nothing.

You are something.

You are the journey.

Your path begins today.

~ This book is **your** guide ~

Traditions and Transitions

Have you ever noticed the true beauty of the sky?

Have you ever noticed the splendor of the ocean as it embraces the earth while touching and creating the horizon so near, yet so far away? Have you ever seen the beauty of rolling hills that seem to go on peacefully... forever... but actually stop somewhere along the bottom of the sky?

Have you ever seen the majestic walls of a sheer mountainside as it connects the heights of the heavens with the depths of the earth?

Each one of these magnificent "scapes" (seascapes, landscapes, natural skyscrapers, and the sky itself) has a profound beauty all by itself.

However, the **grandest** beauty is found where the earth meets the sky, where the sky meets the sea, and where the thunderous seas meet the defining shores of transient rock, soft sand, and every man.

It is at these junctures where an absolute and true transition occurs.

Moreover, it is at these junctures where one form of nature complements the other while simultaneously conquering the same.

Likewise, your grandest beauty is when you are in the midst of a transition. And **know** this:

You are always in the midst of transition!

The question is:

What are your two states of transition?

From *what condition* are you transitioning?

And, most importantly, *to* *what condition are you currently headed*? Where are you going?

As you read these words, your old life is gone. All those things you did before today – do not exist. So, if you are at the top of the world, be careful!

On the other hand, if you are at the bottom of the proverbial valley, staring up at the well-known mountain of life, take a deep breath and boldly proclaim your transition. Accept this miraculous intersection between your distant past and prosperous future.

Accept these two facts:

1. **Your past has helped to create you;**
2. **Your past has almost nothing to do with who you can become.**

Your ideal future does *not* depend on your past.

Your ideal future depends solely on the present.

Your ideal future depends solely on YOU.

Part 2: What's in a Word?

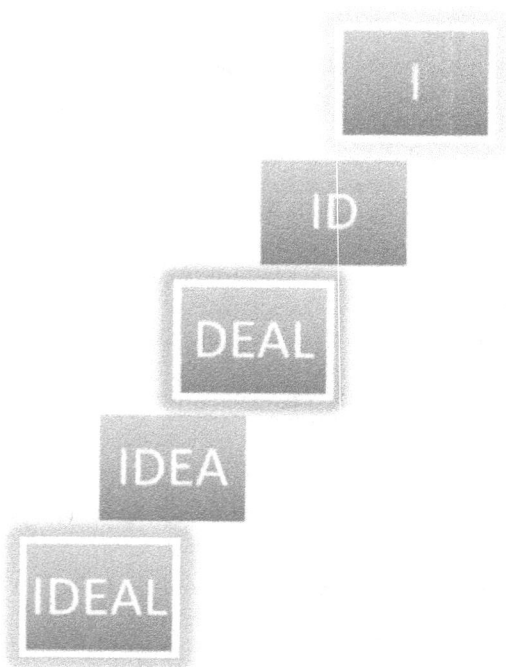

What's in a word?

IDEAL

---

i·de·al *(noun)*

1. Conception of perfection or excellence.
2. An ultimate object of endeavor. A goal.
3. An honorable or worthy principle or aim.

The word *Ideal* is a curious combination of several, very important, smaller words. Invest a moment and focus on the four other specific words available within the word *ideal*:

1. I
2. ID
3. IDEA
4. DEAL

Also, please note the title of this book is not

~ *The Perfect* ~

Your conception of something in absolute perfection is probably remarkably different than my self-made concept of what something is in its state of absolute perfection. Likewise, *your* concept of **The Ideal** is undoubtedly vastly different than *my* concept of **The Ideal.**

So... while we can probably both agree that a perfect life is impossible to achieve, we can also agree that achieving **The Ideal** life is something we all desire. It is an idea whose time has come.

The brain is a marvelous muscle...

IDEA

i·de·a *(noun)*

1. Thought or conception that exists in the mind.
2. A product of mental activity.
3. An opinion, conviction, or principle.

Before you were born into this world, your brain started directing everything from acids to zygotes. Your brain tells you what hurts, helps, and hinders your path through life. Your brain also holds your mind. Your mental mind works within the inner and outer confines of the physical brain, integrating the physical self (the body) with the unseen thoughts that create your sense of self.

Most importantly, your mind *never* stops working. You are *always* thinking. And your (good and bad) thoughts and ideas actually control your emotions.

Your ideas about life actually help **create** the circumstances occurring in your life. Interestingly, two different thoughts cannot occupy the same space within your mind.

Wherever there is a <u>NEGATIVE</u> thought, there can be no positive thought. *And wherever there is a <u>POSITIVE</u> idea, there can be no negative idea.*

For which type of ideas are **you** making space?

So... here's the deal:

DEAL

---

deal *(verb)*

1. To give out as a share or portion.
2. To distribute among several recipients.
3. To sell, administer, or deliver.

Every action you take... Every action you give...

Everything you do is actually a **deal** between your ideas and your body. Every physical act you do in this world is a direct manifestation of your thoughts, your ideas, and your agreement to deal those thoughts into the world of the people around you. Your actions represent the deal between your mind and your body... between your inner world and the outer world.

As the dealer deals selected cards from the deck, you deal selected thoughts from your mind within.

Which ideas are you (literally) bringing into reality? What deals are you making with yourself?

---

deal *(noun)*

1. A bargain, transaction, or agreement.
2. A particular type of treatment received.
3. Treatment resulting from an agreement.

The Id is...

> **Id** *(noun)*
>
> **1.** Inborn behavior responsive to specific stimuli.
> **2.** Techniques and theories from Sigmund Freud.
> **3.** Part of the mind where psychic activity occurs.

The *Id* is arguably that part of your self that makes up the very core of who you really "are."

Without going into significant academic or psychoanalytical detail, let's just say that neurologist Sigmund Freud defined the *id* as *"uncoordinated instinctual trends..."* the absolute truest, most instinctual part of who you really are.

In general, the **Id** wants whatever feels good at the time, with no consideration for the reality of the situation. In today's world, most people are more familiar with Freud's concept of the **ego**, which he defined as the "organized and realistic part of the psyche." *

For the purpose of this book, just remember that the *Id* is the part of your deep, deep self – that part of you that, perhaps, even **you** don't understand sometimes.

---

* Definitions adapted from The American Heritage® Dictionary of the English Language, Fourth Edition. (2003). Retrieved August 21 2011 from http://www.thefreedictionary.com

"I" am...

I *(pronoun)*

1. Used to refer to oneself as the speaker or writer.
2. The self.
3. The ego.

Thus far, we have reviewed definitions for *ideal, idea, deal,* and the *id.* **And then there is you...**

You are the "**I**" in the *Ideal*
You are the "**I**" in the *Idea*
You are the "**I**" in the *Id*
You are the "**I**" in the *I*

You make the "Deal"

This entire book is based upon the notion that you (and *only* you) determine what your ideal state of being is. You are the *only* person who has the capability to define, start, and complete your ideal.

You are the *only* person who understands your best idea (this is called ***The Ideal***). You are the *only* person who can select from all the bad, good, better, and best ideas in your mind. *Only* you.

You are the only person who can make the transaction and *seal the deal* to bring your best ideas out of your head and into your reality.

You are the only person
who can make an **agreement** between
your thoughts and actions.

You are the only person who truly **knows** you!

You are the only person
who hears your thoughts as they are developed.

You are the only person
who can be referred to as *"I"* by you.

When you say *"I,"* you are talking about only you.

When you say **"I,"** you are
speaking your internal thoughts, from the "Id."

When you say, **"I will,"** you are making an
agreement between your thoughts and actions.

When you act, you are dealing with the world.

Whenever you do anything,
you are dealing a new reality into existence.

Whenever you do anything,
you are transforming your ideas into reality.

If you want an ideal life, simply seek to transform
only the best ideas into reality.

If you want to transform only the best ideas,
focus on the *best* ideas. Here's the deal:

Every action in life starts with a thought.
Every thought is born from an idea.

Focus on the best ideas to achieve an ideal life.

Four Little Questions

What is your current challenge in life?

What is preventing you from achieving your wildest dreams? What is keeping you from reaching your highest goals? What do you *really* want to achieve with your life?

What are the speed bumps along your path in life?

Do you honestly know what is truly keeping you on the track of distress and off the path of success?

What specific people or events are you unsuccessfully grappling with right now?

How should you face the next few minutes, days, and weeks? How can you get over your current challenges? How can you achieve the ideal life?

Start with four little questions...

1) What if it **is** true?
2) What **can** I do about it?
3) What **will** I do about it?
4) What **am** I doing about it?

1) So what if "it" is true?

What are the **options** regarding your situation?

Of course, there are *realistic* options. And then there are *unrealistic* options.

There are legal options, and there are illegal options.

There are short-term options. And then there are long-term options.

There are several quick fixes and symptomatic treatments.

And then there are real remedies and actual cures.

But with regard to your current challenge...

What options do you really and truly have?

What can **you** do about it?

Ideally, you can resolve it by seeking the best possible solution.

But let's not get ahead of ourselves...

In any situational challenge, before you can seek **The Ideal** solution, you must start with two basic questions. The first of which is...

1) So what if it *is* true?

Let's start with the most basic question: Is it true? Whatever "it" is... is "it" something on which you should spend valuable "mind space"... Or not?

If "it" *is* true, then you can do something,
... or you can do nothing .

If "it" is *not* true, then you are actually **deal**ing with worry, fear, and other invented emotions. Your mind has much better things to do.

So... if the situation is real, the next question is:

2) What can you *really* do about it?

Regardless of what your challenges are...

No matter how tough life looks right now...

Despite the potential consequences of your previous and next few actions, you are always able to respond with a degree of sanity and certainty.

Yes: Regardless of the situation, when it comes to your course of actions, you are still able to stop, evaluate the situation, and choose a response.

You are ***able*** to respond.

Thus, you are response-***able***.

You are "**responseable**" for your actions.

Thus, you are **responsible** for your actions.

No matter what happens in life; no matter how bad things may *seem*; no matter how bad things actually *get*... You are still response-able for your actions. No one else can own YOUR actions. So...

Think carefully about the range of your potential responses as you ask the next question...

3)   What *will* you do about it?

Of all the things you can do, what do you think you will **actually** do (no-kidding, in-real-life)?

If necessary, a more complicated version of this question can be created, destroyed, reinvented, and strewn across the landscape of life.

However, considering the sheer beauty of transitions and tribulations, simplicity is best paired with more of the same.

In other words, if you think an ideal resolution is best arrived at by engineering some complicated scheme, or by intricately dissecting the potential results to see how you and your interests are best served in the end result... ultimately your complicated schemes will result in a complicated solution... usually one big fat **complicated** mess.

On the other hand, by keeping the range of possibilities simple and straightforward, you will most likely end up with a simple solution.

Sounds "*sillily*" simple, right?

Well... it's more like **super** simple.

So as you move forward in this book, reading deeper and deeper into the concept of *The Ideal*, please try to remember the four simple questions.

These four little questions deserve four little answers. Complicating the questions by providing complex answers will not get you to *The Ideal.* However, the last of these four little questions will launch you directly forward...

4) What *are* you doing about it?

In the realistic quest for an ideal situation, this is literally the million-dollar question. Yes, this is literally a million-dollar question. In fact, let's call it a billion-dollar question.

Actually... let's call it a gazillion-dollar question!

Why? Again, the answer is simple:

There is nothing more valuable than now.

Think about it: Which moment of last year would you trade in for right now? Which of the last four years would you trade for the next four years?

Which of the next sixty minutes would you give up for a million, billion, gazillion dollars?

In reality, you cannot put a price on this one specific moment in time (right here; right now).

There is nothing more valuable than now.

How can I make such a blanket observation?

Quite simply:
Other than right now...
Absolutely nothing else exists!

So... regarding your challenges...

1) What if "it" *is* true?
2) What *can* you do about it?
3) What *will* you do about it?

But most importantly...

What are YOU *doing* about it?

What very real, tangible, and visible actions are you doing today, to resolve your very real issues?

What are you doing to educate yourself on the range of existing options? What are you truly *thinking* about doing?

What have you already done to transform your thinking into linking?

What *are* you doing to link your current thoughts with your (next) actions?

What are you doing to ensure complete, fulfilled answers to all four little questions?

1) What if it *is* true?
2) What *can* I do about it?
3) What *will* I do about it?
4) What *am* I doing about it?

From what condition are you transitioning?

And, more importantly, *to what condition* are you currently headed? What are you *doing* about it?

Here's the Idea:
Only you control you. Other people may influence you. However, when it comes to you, the most powerful person in the world is you.

Here's the Deal:
The only difference between the "you of five years from now"... and the "you of today" is now.

*What **are** you doing about it **now**?*

Part 3: Three Little Words

△ △ △

If there were three little words
that could deliver
one magic cure...

What would be those words?

*What would be **your** cure?*

No magic cures

As you move from the *less-than-ideal* life to a life far beyond what you once **thought** you could have, remember one central point:

There are **no magic cures.**

These three little words are the first of several three-little-word combinations listed within the pages of this simple little book. Though entirely simplistic in terms of the requirements to understand... achieving **The Ideal** is not accomplished by simply waving a magic wand around your head, saying three little words... or clicking your heels together and closing your eyes to the reality of the situation.

If you are convinced there is a hidden secret, and you want to continue looking for a magic cure, look in the mirror. Look deep into the soul of that sole person staring back at you. Those eyes lead to the soul that will prepare your thoughts, clear your mind, and pave your path to **The Ideal** life.

If there were a doctor or a priest who could cure or get rid of other people who "make you sick," there would soon be many other people taking the place of those banished souls who have made your life miserable up to now. So above all else... you must remember one central point:

There are no magic cures.

Ones and Zeros

Computers are almost everywhere these days. At the heart of most late-model cars is a very sophisticated computer. Cars with computers can perform some rather amazing feats. Some cars can automatically sense and act upon the best time to shift from one gear to another, saving the owner hundreds of dollars on the cost of fuel.

Even more amazing, cars can now literally parallel park themselves without the driver's assistance.

Computers now allow us to choose among hundreds of thousands of television shows and movies. Computers and digital music now allows us to buy almost every song ever recorded... via online music stores. That's millions of songs at your fingertips - accessible at this very moment.

And computers now allow us to launch spacecraft and subsequently view some of the most spectacular spheres in our solar system. In fact, computers onboard satellites now allow us to see planets spinning far beyond the setting sun.

This book you are reading was created on a computer in Hawaii, then transferred to hundreds of other computers on the Internet... to a company in Tennessee that printed and shipped this book to the location where you purchased *The Ideal*.

Perhaps the most amazing fact about computers is that the ***most*** *sophisticated computer* in the world is still based on the same decision process of the ***least*** *sophisticated computer.* **All computer algorithms are based on several iterations of one simple question:** *Is the data a '1' or a '0'?*

Sure, there are billions of calculations per second performed by today's computers. Yet, the same basic question applies: *Is the data a '1' or a '0'?* If the data is a '1,' the computer does one thing. If the data is a '0,' the computer "decides" to do something totally different... **this** or **that**.

And when computer programmers combine millions and billion choices between *this or that*, they have the collective data (program), to enable cars to parallel park without the aid of drivers.

When programmers combine millions and billions of different (1 or 0) decisions, programmers actually create a decision process that decides whether or not to send a spaceship to the moon, to Saturn, or somewhere in-between. Literally every decision is "this or that." And if the programmers want **this** to happen, they simply re-program the software to **do this** and **not do that**.

And when **you** combine billions of decisions, you arrive in life where you are now. You are facing decisions once again. However, with this book, you now have the data to move beyond any and every deal. You, too, can re-program your life.

More importantly, you will soon have the data to take you places where you never thought possible.

But in this case, the question will not be...

"Is the data a '1' or a '0'?"

You are not a computer. However, like a computer, you make binary decisions. Your decisions take you **this way** or **that way**... never both ways.

The question is: What will you do with the data?

What will you do with the information gained from this book? Will you use the information to launch far beyond this intersection of space and time? Or will you choose to simply read this book as if it were meant for pure entertainment?

The computer program, when complete, facilitates the phenomenal achievement of certain long, laborious, and previously impossible tasks. Have we underestimated the computer's simplicity of one specific decision to do **this** or **that**?

If something was previously thought to be impossible, but has since become possible because of a new invention... was it ever really *impossible*? *Or did we simply forget that inventions are merely thoughts that have been converted into reality?*

What else are we humans doing that reflects a continual disregard for the sheer significance of repetitive simplicity? You, as a member of the human race, must decide what's possible for you.

Can you invent **The Ideal** life? The choice is yours.

Choose wisely.

Knowledge versus Wisdom

As you read the next few pages, you will probably come across a thought or three that you have heard, read, or said once before. *Good for you!*

However, let's not confuse your great knowledge with your great lack of wonderful wisdom. You could very well be the most knowledgeable person in the world. But if you don't use your knowledge, all that information in your head is being wasted. Are you willing to admit this?

Compare the meanings of knowledge and wisdom:

---

knowl·edge *(noun)*

1. The state or fact of knowing.
2. Familiarity, awareness, or understanding.
3. The sum or range of what has been learned.

---

wis·dom *(noun)*

1. The ability to think and act utilizing knowledge, experience, understanding, and insight.

Here's the Idea:
*Wisdom is the **application** of knowledge.*

Here's the Deal:
*Education is the only asset that no one can take from you. Learn all you can; but be absolutely sure to use your knowledge, or risk losing it. Remember: knowledge is not power until it is applied. When you use knowledge, you instantly become wise. Learn from this book. More importantly, **do what it says!***

As you invest time reading this book, you will begin to see a whole new world. You will learn fundamental concepts upon which all life and thought are based.

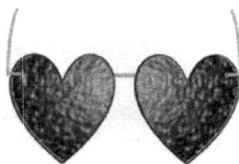

Some of the concepts will be new and exciting. On the other hand, as you read *The Ideal*, a few great, personal ideas will leap from the depths of your own soul, from the back of your own mental mind, and from the far reaches of your wildest dreams.

In this section, *Three Little Words*, there are several micro-chapters written as a foundation to the step-by-step guide at the end of *The Ideal*. Each micro-chapter includes straightforward Truths upon which *The Ideal* roadmap is built. Additionally, there are two simple assertions at the end of each micro-chapter:

> 1. *Here's the Idea*
> 2. *Here's the Deal*

In these statements is an implied course of action: grasp the idea, and fully understand the deals we make as we gallop along the stony road of life.

Following each micro-chapter is a "thought-space." This *thought-space* is comprised of first-person statements and a few blank lines. The *thought-space* is written in the "first person" so you can read it from **your** point of view... aloud with your voice, or silently within the quiet confines of your mind. I encourage you to read the *thought-space* pages aloud. There is something magical that occurs when we speak our sincere intentions to our deepest sense of self.

As you contemplate and consider the advice and directions in the micro-chapters, use the blank lines to capture your immediate thoughts. Your reflective thoughts will serve as milestones and markers on your personal journey. Your introspective thoughts will serve as landmarks to recognize and reaffirm *your* responsive ideas and thoughts after each powerful little chapter.

And though only a few lines are provided as *thought-space,* it is very important that you **invest** a few minutes to jot down your thoughts and, most importantly, your emotions regarding the ideas and ideals in the preceding chapter.

Why is capturing your emotions most important?

Regardless of what you **know** to be true, many of your decisions are based on how you *feel*.

And as you move forward and discover the powerfully integrated Truths in **The Ideal**, you must confront, negotiate, and resolve the dynamic differences between reality and your emotions. When you understand, manage, and negotiate the differences between thought and emotion, you actually create a pathway between knowledge and wisdom; you literally create a solution with the one thing you absolutely, positively control: **YOU**.

Your path to overcoming *anything* begins today. This book is a fact-based roadmap for your journey. And like most roadmaps, this book provides specific guidance on how to get you to your destination. Follow the directions herein, and you will arrive where you truly want to be.

You are the journey.

Choice Equals Power

The power to choose your actions is painfully undervalued, underestimated, and underutilized. In reality, you **choose** every single one of your actions. No one is forcing you to read these words.

You are choosing to read these words.

Aside from birth, you, your self, has chosen to do every single act in your life. And going forward, you, your SELF will **choose** every single act. Indeed, our choices are usually based on a decision *process*. And sometimes fear, family, friends, and foe influence our decision processes.

Before reading the next page...
You must accept this fundamental point:
You control you. No one else controls you.

Other people may *influence* you. Other people may influence *your* behavior. Other people may influence *your* decisions. Other decisions and outcomes may influence, limit, or expand your choices and associated decisions. However...

You are the main supervisor of you.

You are the ultimate director of you.

You are the powerful president of you.

You are the earthly god of you.

Accordingly, **you** are in control of **you**.

And, as director, president, and god of your self, you have the ultimate power over you. People may influence you. But no one can make you do *anything*. No one controls *you*. You control you.

As soon as you think (or believe) that other people have power over you, that thought becomes reality... and they instantly have power over you.

If you have a job, no one is forcing you to work. You have elected to have a job in order to achieve a certain quality of life. In essence, people who have jobs have accepted the understanding that a good day's work provides a good day's pay. Cumulatively speaking, a week's worth of a good day's pay equals a decent paycheck. When we *choose* to work, we are accepting the **deal** that we will be paid for our work. We then adapt to that **deal** by choosing to work. By accepting and adapting to this **deal**, we receive a financial exchange for our labor. We work to get money.

But don't forget the title of this micro-chapter....

~ Choice equals Power ~

If you have a job, you *choose* to work. Working provides the ***power*** to buy things. Your choice to work gives you buying ***power***. And... let's not forget that our main job in life is to survive.

So here's a good question: If your main job in life is to survive, what are you *choosing* to do in order to increase the likelihood of your survivability? What are you doing *today* to ensure your life is better **tomorrow** than it was **yesterday**?

Are you locked into a daily struggle for everyday survival by choosing to do the *"same stuff; different day?"* What seemingly mundane choices comprise or compromise your lifestyle?

Are you choosing the best options for your life?

Or like many people, are you *choosing* to **give** your power to other people, events, and situations?

Do you **blame** other people, events, and situations for your current lifestyle? Seriously... do you?

Your answer to that question may have significant meaning to you. And to be sure, it seems that bad things often happen to good people like you.

However, regardless of your situation... regardless of how you arrived here, *you still have the awesome power of choice.*

You are the one who chooses how to move on from here. Of course, there are some people who refuse to believe that we, ourselves (our *selves*), have the ultimate power over our SELF. Those people have already chosen to give their power to other people, events, and situations.

Remember:

As soon as you think or believe people have power over you, that thought becomes reality, and they instantly have power over you.

As you continue reading, here's something to consider: Up until now, your birthplace, your family, your childhood, and other experiences have quite a bit to say about who you *are*.

On the other hand, relatively speaking, all those things have little or nothing to say about who you can **become.** **You** have the most to say about that!

Here's the Idea:
Only you control you. Other people may influence you. However, when it comes to you, the most powerful person in the world is you.

Here's the Deal:
Astronauts don't get lucky; they choose their ideal profession; and they go for it. It may take a while, but astronauts ultimately shoot for the stars and reach the moon.

Likewise, you have the power to literally create the next minute, month, and mindset. And a lot depends on whether or not you see the world as a mountain or a molehill.

In reality, the best way to predict the future...

... is to create it...

You create your ideal.

Before reading anything else, accept one true fact:

In life, we can play the role of **creator** or **victim.**

Ultimately, only you **decide** which role to play.

To achieve *The Ideal* life, I must understand...
Choice Equals Power

I now understand that, aside from birth, I have chosen to do every single act in my life. And for the rest of my life, I will continue to choose every act. I have the power to choose. Therefore, I am powerful. I am in control of my choices. Therefore, I am powerful. In the past, I felt like I was controlled by events, people, or fears like:

_____

_____

_____

_____

Today, I am ready to fill my tank with my own sense of personal power. Today, I choose to see myself as a creator of solutions instead of a victim of circumstances or previous choices. Today, I accept the Truth that no one else can give me my ideal life. I now believe, understand, and know that the best way to predict the future is to create it. Today, I will start creating my ideal life by:

_____

_____

_____

_____

_____

_____

Accept. Adapt. Achieve. ®

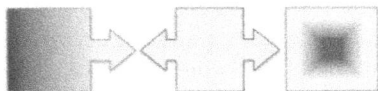

These three little words apply every single day. No matter what the situation; no matter how bad things seem to be; no matter how bad things really are... you must still accept and deal with the reality of the situation. *Accept. Adapt. Achieve.* ®

You must become (and always remain) response-able. And the best way to remain response-able is to see the situation for *what it is.*

To effectively begin changing your reality, you must first **become aware** of your reality.

After awareness, you are faced with the choice to accept or deny reality. Awareness allows acceptance. Being response-able allows you to adapt effectively.

Accept, adapt, and then achieve your goals!

Here's the Idea:
*Whether change is good or bad is entirely dependent on how **you** feel and think about it. Regardless, you can't change what has happened.*

Here's the Deal:
Acceptance is the key to unlocking the door to achieving The Ideal life. Consider the opposite of Accept. Adapt. Achieve... deny, maintain, fail.

To achieve *The Ideal,* I must...
Accept. Adapt. Achieve. ®

To achieve my ideal life, I need to honestly assess what issues, people, or events I am not accepting in my life. What am I in denial about?

Regardless of what has happened, I choose to live in the time of today instead of yesterday. I choose to accept the *fact* that I cannot change what has already happened. I now see how the power of choice and acceptance can change my life forever.

I feel like my life changed forever when:

_____

_____

My biggest challenge in this area is: _____

_____

_____

I think I can accept the fact that I can't change:

_____

_____

Here's what I **can** do: _____

_____

_____

_____

Everything. Anything. *Your*thing.

You can't do everything.

In today's technologically integrated world, so many things happen almost instantaneously. We click a button and someone a thousand miles away receives an electronic letter or a picture. Through the invention of cell phones, we can call almost anyone from almost anywhere. And because of the availability of some pretty fabulous electronic gadgetry, we can do almost anything anywhere.

Of course, that last statement is not true at all. We *can't* do almost anything anywhere.

In fact, in some aspects of our lives, technology has actually reduced our ability get things done. Computers, cell phones (which are actually little computers), music devices (more little computers), televisions (in and out of the vehicle, home, and office), and various other attention-getters actually decrease our ability to consider, develop, and improve upon our ideal landscape.

Instead of doing almost anything anywhere, many of us are trying to do **everything**. And because we think it's ok to try to do everything, we seem to be willing to do **anything**.

Making matters worse... because we are so accustomed to answering *this*, watching *that*, clicking *here*, switching *there*... some people actually feel disengaged from our world when their inbox is empty; when their "reality" shows are not currently on; or when their cell phone is not ringing, texting, or downloading!

How did this happen?

How did we independently become so dependent on the interdependence of our dependencies? How did we lose sight of the significant importance of our independence?

How did we get to the point where we know so much about technology and yet we know so little about ourselves?

> Beginning today...
> ...forget "everything."

And before you do anything... simply take some time today and think about **YOUR**thing. What is it that **YOU** want to do?

Why is this important?

Let's review the obvious facts:
1. You *can't* do everything.
2. You *can* do almost anything.
3. You *choose* your thing.

To try to do *everything* is simply impossible. And since it's impossible to do *everything*, we should focus on and *choose* to do a smaller set of *everything*. The hundred-thousand-dollar question is: Which things should you choose to do?

From what part of everything *can* you choose?

For many people, the list of potential and possible lifestyles is endless.

From apple farmer to zookeeper... from archer to Zoroastrian... many people are physically unlimited in their ability to choose and achieve certain occupations and professions in life.

However, many of us are physically challenged and simply cannot do things that others can do.

Quadriplegics don't usually physically run with their legs; blind people don't usually read with their eyes; and you don't usually (*insert your real or perceived physical or mental limitation here*).

Perhaps the list of things that people can't physically do is enormously long. Perhaps you feel (or know) there are significant and severe limitations on what you can personally do.

Aside from your long list of limitations, if you really think about it... you can probably still do just about *anything*.

Here's the Idea:
*In reality, your list of limitations pales when compared to the universe of things you **can** do.*

Here's the Deal:
*Once you accept the fact that you can't do everything, you will more clearly understand and see what you **can** do. You can do almost anything. But what do you really **want** to do?*

To achieve *The Ideal*, I must consider...
Everything. Anything. MYthing.

I am a unique person.

There is no other person in the whole world that can do the collective things that I can do. Some people are amazingly pretty. That is the gift they have been given, and it is the gift they bring to the world. Some people are amazingly smart. Others and their seemingly amazing gifts do not alarm me. Today, I seek and speak my special contribution to the world. I enjoy doing these three things:

1. _____

2. _____

3. _____

I would really like to: _____

_____

Here's what I **can** do: _____

_____

Here's what I **am** doing: _____

_____

_____

_____

_____

Life Changing Events

Life-changing events occur everyday.

Interestingly, when people hear the phrase "life-changing events," they often think of a negative event or experience. And yes, death, divorce, and debilitating diseases are clear examples of life-changing events. However, there are also good, positive life-changing events. The birth of a child, a promotion at work, and meeting your soul mate are all clear examples of a life-changing event.

As you delve into the next few chapters of *The Ideal*, give some thought to the possibility that this book is actually changing your life.

Wow! That's a rather bold statement coming from the pages of this little blue book! Entire civilizations and countries have teetered on far greater, stronger words and promises than "this book will change your life."

However, this book is not out to change the world. And it's not out to change you. Only *you* can change you. This book **can** change your thoughts.

Here's the Idea:
Your life changes every single minute of every day.

Here's the Deal:
If you believe this book will change your life, it will.

To achieve *The Ideal*, I must remember...
Life Changing Events are good things, too!

If I could change one specific thing in my life right now, I would change:

_____

_____

I feel like I can change my life if I can just:

_____

_____

Here's what I **can** do: _____

_____

_____

Here's what I **will** do: _____

_____

_____

Here's what I **am** doing: _____

_____

_____

_____

_____

If and When

Have you ever said, *"If this happens, I will..."*

How many times did that particular event actually happen, but you ultimately decided **not** to do what you *said* you would do?

The *"If-and-When"* statement can be a good starting point when setting goals. Many planned events and situations in our lives depend on other events and situations. And despite our best efforts to plan, sometimes things happen outside our span of control. Sometimes those external events affect our planned, predicated events.

When this happens, don't despair, and don't misinterpret those influential, external events as "controlling" your decisions about your life.

Remember: Plans are only thoughts. When you place those thoughts on paper, those plans are still thoughts until the events actually happen.

Here's the Idea:
If and when situations change your plans, simply change your thoughts and the associated plans.

Here's the Deal:
*If and when you proactively expect things to change, you will accept and adapt to the changes immediately. Plan for change; it **will** happen!*

To achieve *The Ideal*, I will focus on now...
If and When is not part of my plan.

If my life ended today, and then I was subsequently given another life beginning with today, what would I do differently?

Regardless of what has happened in my life, I am living today. Yesterday, yesteryear, my *yesterlife* and all those things that have already happened will never happen again. No matter how much I want to change yesterday or tomorrow... I am powerless to change those imaginary memories and dreams.

On the other hand, I am tremendously powerful when it comes to choosing right here and now to say to my SELF: *I am not waiting for another "if or when."* **Today I am starting:**

_____

_____

_____

_____

_____

_____

_____

Beginning today, and starting every morning *before* I get out of bed, I will say to my SELF:

~ My new life *began* today ~

Priorities. Propensities. Presentations.

3, 2, 1

These three aspects of our lives affect everything.

Priorities. From the time we wake up, we prioritize our day. We prioritize the order of making breakfast and getting dressed. We prioritize the status of friends, family, and foe.

Propensities. These are the habits and routines that keep us on our current path. Interestingly, our daily habits actually work to *prevent* us from changing anything in our highly patterned life. Our propensities are already formed, but they are also dynamic, and subject to change at any time.

Presentations. Often referred to as perspectives, presentations are the physical, mental, and social lenses of our True Self. More than mere perspectives, presentations are literally how we present things to each other and ourselves.

Everything we do is affected by how we decide to prioritize our day, our week, and our life. Moreover, our propensities (our habits) help ensure today is quite a bit like yesterday. In fact, some scientists estimate as much as 80% of our daily activities can be considered *habitual*.

But we rarely see our habits and ourselves. We have a self-perception that is skewed by denial.

Similarly, we also have a world-perception. And like self-perception, world-perception is an awareness and viewpoint of the characteristics comprising the world... as you and I see it.

Our viewpoints are continuously evolving, constantly being refined by our everyday experiences. But what is a "**presentation?**"

Similar to perspectives, *presentations* are *how we present and represent the facts to ourselves and to others.* Some might argue that a *presentation* is the same thing as a perspective or a perception. But these two words only cover part of the story.

Self-perspective, relates to how we see ourselves.

Perception relates to how we see the world.

But *presentations* relate to perspective *and* perception, as well as a third element: How we intend for the world to see us.

This third element specifically relates to how we present ourselves to the world. Interestingly, self-perception is simply another *presentation*: It's how we *present* our self to our self. It's what we tell ourselves about our self. Likewise, world-perception is also another *presentation*: It's how we present the world to our self. It's what we tell ourselves about the world.

So... there are three presentations that we make as we interact with the world and ourselves. Two of these presentations are mere perspectives.

However, the third presentation is just that: A pure presentation – a way of presenting and representing ourselves – to the world around us.

All three presentations are distinctly different; yet each one affects the other. All three presentations converge into a great recipe to create, re-create, improve, amend, and make the person that is you. Most importantly, **each presentation directly affects your priorities and your propensities.**

So if you want to change your priorities, simply change your presentations. And if you really want to change your propensities (your habits), simply align your three types of presentations.

> **Presentation of your self to your self**
> *Self Perception*
>
> **Presentation of the world to your self**
> *World Perception*
>
> **Presentation of your self to the world**
> *Fake & Failing or Fact-based & Fruitful*

If your presentations are misaligned or inaccurate, you are **deal**ing with a false reality. And when you are **deal**ing with a false reality, you are **deal**ing with lies. When **deal**ing with lies, you are **deal**ing with a fantasyland, a land that does not really exist (And a nonexistent place cannot be changed).

On the other hand, when you begin to align all aspects of your world (your view of your self; your view of the world; and your presentation of your self to the world), you are dealing with reality.

Moreover, to truly change your habits and priorities, you must **see** the need to change your habits and priorities. In order to **see** the need to change your habits and priorities, you must have the proper perspective.

If your view of the **world** is skewed away from reality, you must re-align your presentation with reality. If your view of your **self** is skewed away from reality, you must re-align your presentation.

If your **presentation of your self** *is skewed away from reality, you must work to align that presentation (of your self to the world) with reality.*

After aligning your true self with self-perceptions and self-presentations, you will begin to experience real change. By illuminating and sharing your true self with the world, your life will begin to change in ways that are simply unimaginable to you right now.

Are you ready for a fact-based and fruitful life?

Beginning today, you can get rid of every fear, every fake projection of self, and every misaligned pattern of life. How? Simply start the alignment of presentations. Starting today, accept one true fact: There is only one true perception: the Truth.

Here's the Idea:
Together we'll stand, the mighty and tall.
   Divided by shams, the mighty will fall.

Make the choice, and blend the three:
   ...parts of self, they must agree.

Here's the Deal:
Your priorities, propensities, and presentations can work with each other; or they can work against each other. When you dabble in half-truths, you are really dabbling in half-lies, both of which result in a half-enjoyable life. When you seek the Absolute Truth, you are better prepared to see, understand, and absolutely **know** *what can truly become of you.*

To achieve *The Ideal*, I will focus on aligning...
Priorities. Propensities. Presentations.

A key cornerstone of an ideal life is alignment.
To facilitate growth from where I am, I need a
solid foundation with a newly aligned me.

I will not underestimate this significant point: My foundation is either weak from misalignment... or strong in alignment. *If* and *when* I align all three presentations (the presentation of my SELF to myself; my SELF to the world; and the presentation of the world to me), a solid foundation is created. I will not wait until *if* or *when* something happens.

I will start the alignment of myself - today.

I choose to accept the ***fact*** that I cannot live an ideal life until my presentations are aligned. I now see how the power of alignment changes lives!

I am willing to accept the **fact** that my presentations are NOT aligned. For example:

_____

_____

_____

_____

Here's what I **can** do to achieve alignment:

_____

_____

Choose your superlative.

Everything else, by definition, ...follows.

---

su·per·la·tive *(noun)*

1. Of the highest order, quality, or degree.
2. Surpassing or superior to all others.

Remember: The only one who can make you do anything is **you**. You have the power to choose your next step, next path, and next destination.

Choose carefully; no one else has total power over the awesome being of you - except for you! Wow!

When you choose **your** superlative, you are proclaiming that nothing else can topple the single most important thing in your life, your true self.

You matter more than anything.

Self. Environment. Mission.

What is your idea of your self? What do you think about your environment? What is your idea of your mission in life? No matter where one goes in life, three basic concepts exist: *self, environment, and mission.* A few common examples are below

If you are a father, this Truth applies:
- Self: Father
- Environment: Family
- Mission: Protect & Provide

If you are a mother, this Truth applies:
- Self: Mother
- Environment: Family
- Mission: Protect & Nurture

If you are an employee, this Truth applies:
- Self: Employee
- Environment: Workplace
- Mission: What you do

If you are a teacher, this Truth applies:
- Self: Teacher
- Environment: School
- Mission: Teach

If you are a police officer, this Truth applies:
- Self: Peace Officer
- Environment: Community
- Mission: Protect and Serve

If you are a doctor, this Truth applies:
- Self: Physician
- Environment: Hospital
- Mission: Heal

When referencing the three basic Truths of *self, environment, and mission...* which of the three is most important when determining **The Ideal** ?

What is your mission in life? Is your mission the most important thing you will ever do?

Or on the other hand, is the **environment** supremely more important than the mission and the self that is you?   After all, the environment ultimately affects everyone, right?

In reality, no matter what environment you are in; no matter what your mission is... you, your self, is always much more important than anything else.

~ Without you, there could be no you ~

And without you, there is no mission, regardless of the environment!   Thus, in order to focus on achieving **The Ideal**, let's focus on the Truth that matters most: your SELF.

But are **YOU** true to **SELF**?

Here's the Idea:
Your True Self matters more than your mission or the uncertainties of an uncontrollable environment.

Here's the Deal:
Know this: You literally change the world wherever you go. And though you cannot control the environment, you can make it your mission to influence the happiness of others.   You find happiness where you give it.   Give happiness and you will affect and influence your own happiness.

Your mission: Choose **HOW** to deal with today.

**To achieve *The Ideal*, I admit that *I* matter!
*Self. Environment. Mission.***

**Let's be honest here.   The most important
person in the whole wide world is me.**

Even if I am not the most benevolent person in the
world, I am still the most important person in the
world. Does my importance to my SELF mean I
am a selfish person? Absolutely not!

Without me, there would be no me.   Such a
statement may seem silly. Nonetheless, it is a true
statement. I must remember:

> At this point, my beliefs don't really matter.
> What I ***know*** is what really matters.

I need to *know* that I matter. I need to know that I
am a very valuable gift to this world. I need to
know that the world needs me to discover my
passion. I see how the knowledge of my true self
can change my life and the lives of other people.

If I could **choose** my own specific mission in life
(and somehow be guaranteed of my success at
that chosen mission), I would definitely choose to:

_____

_____

_____

Here's what I **can do** to get started on my mission:

_____

_____

Get. Give. Grow.

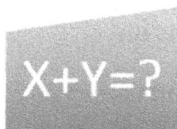

Quite simply... in life, you get what you give.

Here's the deal: When you give peace and joy to your neighbor, the same will be dealt to you. *Knowing* this, will you give your neighbor miles of smiles or piles of vile? It's also worth noting that the timing of your deals is not yours to follow.

In other words, it's **not** a good idea to keep a little black book of all the peace and joy owed to you. Nor is it a good idea to track all the venom and dirt slopped in your direction. On the other hand, it **is** a good idea to altruistically and cheerfully give what is yours to give. By offering others a smile, you are giving them a small snapshot of happiness. By giving them a picture of happiness, you are investing in their hope and your future.

But how do you really and truly **find** happiness? The answer is amazingly simple. You get what you give. Give happiness, and you will certainly find happiness. Give it, and you will grow happy.

Here's the Idea:
What goes around really does come around.

Here's the Deal:
You can't give what you don't have. First find your initial stash of happiness. Where is this happiness?

Read the next chapter.

If I want to achieve *The Ideal*, I will...
Get. Give. Grow.

Maybe the old adage is right: *What goes around comes around.* **Interestingly, many of the world religions and philosophies embrace *The Ideal* of getting back what we give out.**

Regardless of whether or not I believe in a Higher Power, I should at least be aware of the fact that my interaction with others is actually a **deal** between my thoughts, my actions, and all the other people of the world. If I am the **deal**er of my life's deck of cards, what am I dealing to others?

How am I dealing *with* the world?

I choose to accept the *fact* that I am connected to everyone else in this seemingly disconnected world. I can see how the power of giving can change my life as well the lives of so many others!

I **feel** like I can definitely grow in this area by:

_____

_____

_____

_____

_____

Here's what I **will** do: _____

_____

_____

An Inside Job

When YOU change, the world changes.

As you invest a few more hours, days, and weeks digesting the material in the chapters ahead, keep a very important idea at the top of your mind:

When you change your view of the world...
The world will change its view of you.

Try this little experiment: Wear a pair of flamboyant sunglasses for ONE ENTIRE DAY. As long as the glasses don't affect your health and safety, keep them on your face. No matter who ridicules you, keep the glasses on. No matter what people say or do, keep the glasses on your face.

When you keep the glasses on, you will, of course, see the world differently (from the inside of your head). Interestingly enough, as you see the world differently, people will look at **you** differently. Of course, their reasons for staring at you will be different than the reasons for your new ability to see the world differently... or will they?

The bottom-line Truth: When it comes to you... you *and* everyone you see that day will see your world differently solely because of the glasses.

Likewise, as you use this book to change the lenses through which you view the world...

...the world will change how it sees you.

In accordance with the previous micro-chapter *"Priorities. Propensities. Presentations."* by wearing the unusual glasses, you can change two things:

1. How you present **the world** to **yourself**;
2. How you present **yourself** to **the world**.

Now this may seem like a ridiculous application or example of the micro-chapter on *Priorities, Propensities, and Presentations.* However, it's actually a perfect example of the PPP concept.

If you truly want to achieve **The Ideal**, start by changing your own personal view of the world.

Don't wait for someone to give you the magic cure. Changing your life is an inside job. And once you accept the responsibility of managing your life the way **only you** can manage it, you will immediately begin to adapt to situations quite differently.

Here's the Idea:
Expecting others to change is a critical ingredient in a rotten recipe for disaster. Accepting the magnificence of change as you adapt to a changing world... is a successful formula for dealing with an ever-changing world.

Here's the Deal:
As you turn to the next page of this book, you are making the conscious decision to release expectations of change in other people. You are now aware of the tremendous power to effect immediate change in the most important person in the whole world: You - your one true self.

If you want a quick synopsis of life and an equally quick summary of what *The Ideal* is about...

Take a look at these two descriptive pictures.

In general, if you focus and fill your head with blissful thoughts, when you face challenging or changing situations, you will reach deep into your mind and find similar solutions. *The Ideal* is based on the premise that life is based on what you feed your mind. What do *you* feed *your* mind?

What are the odds that you will pull a happy solution from each of these two "minds" ?

To achieve *The Ideal*, I can see that it really is...
An Inside Job

I am the only person who can make an agreement
between *my* thoughts and *my* actions.

I am the only person who **knows** me!

I am the only person
who hears my thoughts as they are developed.

I am the only person
who can be referred to as *"I"* by me.

When *I* say *"I,"* *I* am talking about only me.

When *I* say, *"I will..."*
I am in agreement with my thoughts and actions.

When *I* act, *I* am *dealing* with the world.

Whenever *I* do anything...
I am transforming *my* ideas into reality.

Whenever *I* do anything...
I am dealing a new reality into existence.

If *I* want ***The Ideal*** life...
I only need to transform **my** best ideas.

If *I* want to ***transform*** my best ideas,
I must <u>focus</u> on the best ideas. Here's the deal:

Every action in life starts with a thought.
Every thought is born from an idea.

I must...

Focus on the best ideas to achieve an ideal life.

Buying and Selling

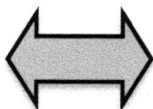

In life, there is always an exchange of this and that.

There are always two sides of the same coin.

There is always you… and then something else.

However, believe it or not: *Everything* is related.

Because everything is related, invest the time and ask yourself, ***"What side of the coin am I on?"***

What am I exchanging with the world? What am I *buying* from people, events, and media as I ***pay*** attention? What am I *selling* to people who are willing to pay me their limited supply of attention? Most importantly, what are they *buying* from me?

Here's the Idea:
Everything you believe is based upon your thoughts or someone else's thoughts given (sold) to you. Everything you say and do has a real, tangible effect on others. Your thoughts affect your actions. Your actions affect many, many other people.

Here's the Deal:
*When you fully accept and truly understand your connection to "now," you will ultimately understand your absolute ability to affect not only today, but also every day connected to "now," especially tomorrow and the weeks, months, and years that follow. What are **you** currently buying and selling?*

The Ideal is really about what I am...
Buying and Selling

What issues really resonate with me? What political party do I align myself to? Why?

What race am I considered? Why? By whom?

What do I tell people about me, my life, and "I"?

Why?

What headline am I selling when I do what I do?

More importantly... why does it matter? To whom does it matter? With whom do I share this information? Is it important to them or only me? In *The Ideal* life, I would like to tell every single person I know these five things:

1. _____

_____

2. _____

_____

3. _____

_____

4. _____

_____

5. _____

_____

Over the Horizon

My life, My love...
    The depth of my soul.
Within, above,
    betwix of your shoals.
There it comes. Here it goes:
The mighty, the many,
    the few that it shows.
Kiss the other,
    but none too soon.
For there I'll get...
    and another will loom.

Here's the Idea:
The magnificent realm of the soul is deeper and wider than the most majestic ocean. Like the returning waves that sweep the vast open sea, the events in our lives are "perfect."

Here's the Deal:
How much of the ocean can we really see? The wave of the east soon greets the west. Likewise, our lives are comprised of trials, trips, and apparent traps. In reality, those traps, trips, and trials are merely tracks of the trail that only you, the traveler, will ever really see – but not fully understand.

I now see *The Ideal* as a flowing wave of life...
Over The Horizon

In many ways, life is like poetry. Some people can read a particular poem and immediately understand and appreciate the poet's dramatic intent and emotional gift. On the other hand, other people can read the exact same poem and actually toss the poem aside in disgust.

How can the world be so powerfully different?

Much like the ocean waves that wrap continuously around the earth, people of the world are connected somehow, some way...

But rarely, if ever, will we see the connection. Our lack of visibility or comprehension of the connection does not mean the connection doesn't exist. The same is true with our view of the world.

In life, we may never fully understand why things *are* the way they *are*. The best we can do is to simply accept, adapt, and then achieve what we can do... while encompassing all that has occurred.

I don't understand (insert your frustrations here):

_____

_____

_____

My biggest challenge in this area is: _____

_____

_____

Today. Tomorrow. Never.

If you started reading **The Ideal** from *Page 1*, you are now almost halfway through this fact-based account on how to achieve **The Ideal** life. You have already been exposed to (or reminded of) several basic truths about life. You have been invited to appreciate *Three Little Words.*

Those *Three Little Words* include the fact that there are *No Magic Cures*, but there is a huge difference between *Knowledge versus Wisdom.* When we use our knowledge, we become wiser, and we implement better choices. *Choice Equals Power.* However, what will you *Accept, Adapt, Achieve*® in life? What will you decide between *Everything, Anything, YourThing*?

In reality, reading this book can be one of your *Life Changing Events If and When* you decide to review your *Priorities, Propensities, and Presentations* about life. As stated in the previous pages, your *Self, Environment,* and *Mission* are all related. And we *Get, Give,* and *Grow* based upon how we improve our lives, which is really *An Inside Job.* Before going any further, consider how much attention you are paying to useless and harmful things. What are you *Buying and Selling* with your attention? What *Over the Horizon* issues are you worried about? Instead of worrying about then and there, focus on today. If you don't start **today**, you probably won't start tomorrow. And if you don't start today or **tomorrow**, you will likely **never** start.

Today. Tomorrow. Now.

The only difference between the **you of today** and the **you of tomorrow** is based on what you are doing right now to change the "you of today."

Remember: **Now** is a continuously moving point on the timeline of your life.

The *now* in the first paragraph on this page is infinitely different than the *now* in this particular sentence. **Now** exists today, right HERE.

There is no "now of tomorrow." There is no "now of yesterday." There is no "now of yesteryear."

There is only **Now**.

Let's get started on **The Ideal** life now.

Here's the Idea:
People spend far too much time worrying about tomorrow, fretting about yesterday, and ultimately wasting away the precious moments of today. This waste of time is not an accidental happenstance. We actively choose how to spend our lives.

Here's the Deal:
As one moment moves into the next moment, your next thought is affected by the thought you have right now. Your next action is based upon your current thought. Start today! Change your mind. Change your thoughts. Change your life!

Okay. I am ready <u>TODAY</u> for *The Ideal*...
Today. Tomorrow. Now or Never...

Unlike yesterday or last month, now I see...

_____

_____

_____

As I look back on the previous chapters of this book, I have learned five very important ideas:

1. _____

_____

2. _____

_____

3. _____

_____

4. _____

_____

5. _____

_____

*~ Today, I **choose** my new life ~*

The Ideal life

Pay Attention Please

What would you do if your cable TV stopped working tonight? What if there was only static fuzz on the screen when you turned on the TV?

Would you check the cable connections? Would you check the electrical cords? Would you call the cable company and demand immediate attention? You could probably spend hours trying to figure out what's wrong with your cable TV, only to discover the television was on the wrong channel!

Yes, there is a huge difference in signals received when placing your television on channel '3' and when placing your television on channel '4.'

Likewise, there is a huge difference in the type of information we *use* when we change the type of information we *receive*. Are you paying attention to the "right" things and people?

~ Pay attention to what you pay attention ~

Here's the Idea:
Everyone has a limited attention span. The world is full of people who are actively demanding your attention. Your attention is much more precious than your money. Don't spend it on divisive topics.

Here's the Deal:
Your attention is actually as precious as time itself.
Your attention is the literal definition of now.

Stop Paying Attention

What is the absolute difference between a Republican and a Democrat? What is the true difference between an American and an Asian? What **one** thing does the Republican need and the Democrat not need? What **one** thing does the American need and the Asian not need?

What can White women do that definitely and distinctively separates their capability from Asian, Hispanic, or Black women? What can **you** do? Whose mother deserves to be loved?

Whose son is better than his, hers, or yours? How much love can we give before we become full of hate? How long must we continue to divide our minds, bodies, and souls according to what someone says about "those" people, "these" politics, and those practically insane ideas that people and politicians perpetuate as you and others pay your attention?

~ Pay attention to what you pay attention ~

Here's the Idea:
We actively choose our music. We actively choose if, when, and what we watch on television. We also passively ingest vast amounts of information.

Here's the Deal:
When you stop paying attention to stupid stuff, you will soon see just how stupid some stuff really is.

**To achieve *The Ideal,* I need my self to…
Pay Attention…**

**What issues, people, or events am I accepting
in my life? Who decides what I do and when I
do those things that I do? Hmmmm… It's me!**

Why do I pay my attention to this or that?

Why do I not like the things that I do not like?

Why do I like the things that I like?

Why do I read books like this?

After reading this micro-chapter, I can see how
other people's definition of other people really
makes no sense at all! I now see that everyone has
a right to think what he or she wants.   The
question is: ***Why*** do they think ***what*** they think?
To whom did they pay their attention? From
whom did they buy their ideas?

**I now understand that my attention is literally
the definition of "right now." Accordingly, I
will stop paying attention to these five things:**

1. _____

2. _____

3. _____

4. _____

5. _____

Literally, the definition of now = my attention.

Start Paying Attention

What would you do if someone gave you $10,000 a day for the rest of your life? How would you spend it? Better yet, what would you do if someone gave you $50,000 a day for the rest of your life? Would it change how you spend your days? Let's take it one step further: What if your daily attention was worth $86,400 per day?

What if you absolutely had to spend a gift of $86,400 every single day… and you could spend it any way you wanted… with one single limitation:

You can't know when that gift will suddenly stop.

Would you spend it carefully? Would you give it away freely and untroubled, despite knowing that the gift could stop any day? Beginning today, I challenge you to accept and understand the fact that your life is a gift. You and I did absolutely nothing to earn it. This great gift of life is exactly 86,400 seconds long every single day. **These gifted seconds may be yours tomorrow. Or on the other hand, this may be the last "time" you ever read such ridiculously truthful words.**

Here's the Idea:
I think you get the idea.

Here's the Deal:
By paying attention to the great gift of life, you are immediately wealthy.

To achieve *The Ideal,* I need my self to...
Start Paying Attention

Wow!

My life is worth 86,400 daily seconds!

Wow!

I have 86,400 seconds to spend every day!

How wisely am I investing my limited seconds?

How foolishly am I spending my limited seconds?

After reading this micro-chapter, I see how my life is made up of so much time! I also see how I have allowed my attention and time to be squandered away on shows, toes, low-blows, this, that, and so many other things. I simply cannot afford to continue paying attention to those things! I now understand the value of life. I value NOW.

I now understand that my attention is literally the definition of "right now." Accordingly, I will start paying attention to these five things:

1. _____

2. _____

3. _____

4. _____

5. _____

My attention is the literal definition of now.

Clean Your Glasses

Day in and day out, we awake to a rising sun, and sleep to the setting same. Day in and day out, we face the choices of life: what to eat, wear, and sleep? This is something **all of us** face every day.

In reality, to survive on this planet, all we really need is food, clothing, and shelter. However...

We are more than mere survivalist on a drifting planet in an infinite universe. We are a mind, body, and a sensitive soul. And we need the minds and bodies of other sensitive souls. And sometimes other people will *purposefully* toss dirt onto our rose-colored glasses as we seek **The Ideal** life. Perhaps you have already tried to start a new life... only to be tricked by the challenges of people, politics, or a particularly cruel person.

What can you do to negate the negativity?

~ Simply clean your glasses ~

Here's the Idea:
The highway is full of bad drivers. Life is full of bad people. Learn to avoid and navigate around them.

Here's the Deal:
Every new second of every minute of every day is totally disconnected from the previous second, minute, and hour. When others toss dirt your way, simply clean yourself off. It is just that simple.

In *The Ideal* world, a good rule is to...
Clean Your Glasses

As the great philosopher Seneca said:
"One should count each day a separate life."

Am I perfect? Of course not!

Accordingly, I should not expect anyone else to be perfect. In fact, instead of expecting my closest friends, family, and foe to be near-perfect people in my ideal world, I should actually love and enjoy them for the flaws, faults, and failings that they have done and will continue to do! No matter how hard I try, I will *never* be perfect. Whether I intend to or not, I will probably end up offending someone, somehow, some day. Likewise, somebody somewhere will likely (knowingly or unknowingly) affect my life in a negative manner.

This is a fact.

Beginning today, I now see that life is a beautiful patchwork of the givin' and the takin', forgivin' and mistakin', all of it real, regardless of the fakin'.

Here's what I **can** do to positively start my day:

_____

_____

Here's what I **will** do to keep my day positive:

_____

_____

Fill Their Glasses

So... if life is full of bad drivers and bad people, **how** can we expect to live **The Ideal** life when negative media, maniacs, and messages of mistrust constantly bombard us? How can we find happiness when happiness seems so elusive and temporary? The answer is so simple... it may surprise you. In fact, the answer might scare you!

The absolute best way to *find* happiness is to simply **give** happiness. Huh? How is this possible? Can I really find happiness right "here?"

Yes! By the time you are finished reading this book, you will fully understand that happiness is not some distant destination or piece of X, Y, Z.

Happiness is something you already have. The big question is: **What are you doing with it – today?**

Here's the Idea:
If I ask you to be happy right now, you can literally decide to place a smile on your face and think happy thoughts. Why wait for me to ask you to do it? Simply decide to do it now.

Here's the Deal:
When you actively decide to "be happy," others see you as happy. When others consistently see you as happy, they expect you to be happy. Instead of expecting others to give happiness to you, raise **their** *expectations and give it to them!*

As I create *The Ideal* world, I will...
Fill Their Glasses

I will try this easy, fun experiment:

As I go through the remainder of my day, I will consciously focus on greeting the next ten people I see with a genuine smile. Regardless of who they are, what they look like, or how they are looking at me, I will simply smile and politely nod my head. This will be fun!

I now see that I can choose to spread happiness, or I can choose to spread sadness. My demeanor can actually be a reflection of how I *want* to feel.

I think I can finally accept: _____

_____

_____

My biggest challenge in this area is: _____

_____

_____

Here's what I **can** do: _____

_____

_____

Here's what I **am** doing: _____

_____

_____

Bigger Than You

So... if we are expected to raise other people's expectations and give happiness to them, **how** can we expect to live **The Ideal** life when less-than-idealistic people draw on our happiness reserves?

First, you must understand that everything... yes... everything is bigger than you. Humbling? Yes!

Relationships are always more important than the individuals in the relationship. By definition, the relationship is **how individuals relate to one another.** Thus, in business, romantic, and social relationships, the individuals must appreciate and respect the relationship more than themselves.

When people think or make themselves more important than the relationship, the relationship **appears** to lose beneficial aspects of integrated exchange. And though there may be ample opportunity for destructive behavior, in general, we must still appreciate the vast connectedness of our self, the environment, and our respective missions. Quite simply... life is bigger than you.

Here's the Idea:
Everything is connected in some way, shape, form, or fashion. Accordingly, the good, the bad, and the ugly are related and in a relationship with you.

Here's the Deal:
Have faith. The Ideal is as close as you think.

In *The Ideal* life, you know some things are...
Bigger Than You

It's true: I am a very important person in this world. However, without all the other people in the world, where would I be? I am actually part of a much larger network of people, places, and positive energy that really does exist on this planet called Earth. Wow!

Looking back over the last five years, I can see that significant changes have occurred in this world. I now realize that I may never really understand why certain things happened the way they did. Somehow, though, I have managed to make it to where I am right here, reading these truthful words. I cannot change what has already happened. But I can see how the power of acceptance can leave yesterday where it is... while bringing my real life to me... right here, right now.

I now see that my life is part of a bigger plan, a bigger journey, and a bigger plot of land. My neighborhood is the world... not just the block.

I think I can finally accept: _____

_____

_____

My biggest challenge in this area is: _____

_____

_____

_____

Take Nothing Personally

So... if everything is connected, and all you need is a little bit of faith, why do good things happen to bad people? And, more importantly, **how** can you expect to live **The Ideal** life when bad things happen to you... especially when you are trying so hard to do the right thing?

The answer is so simple... it may surprise you.

No matter what people may do to you, against you, or for you... don't take it personally. In fact, even if someone does something personally and purposefully to disrespect you, don't take it personally. Sounds too simple, eh?

Well, consider rat poison or drain cleaner.

If someone offered poison to you, would you take it? What if someone offers you a sneezed-on hand, full of viruses? Would you take it? These may sound like simple questions with obvious answers. However, the same principle applies when someone offers you words, actions, or deeds against you: It's a choice. You don't have to accept poisonous words, actions, thoughts, or ideas.

Here's the Idea:
Your # 1 goal should be to maintain an ability to respond. You should always remain response-able.

Here's the Deal:
Whatever "it" is, this, too, shall pass.

In creating *The Ideal* world, I will...
Take Nothing Personally

Why are some people so mean and nasty? Why is there so much evil in the world? When will I finally get the chance to relax and enjoy life? Better yet - when will I get the chance to enjoy watching those evil people get what's coming to them? Wouldn't that be kinda' cool or fun?

Actually... sooner or later, people really do get what they "deserve." Of course, when people are mean to me, I'd actually like to see those people get their share of pain – *immediately*. In reality, life has a way of facilitating balance in a manner that is a tad bit different than what I would prefer.

Some of the poorest people actually have a greater sense of wealth than those people with millions of dollars in the bank. Likewise, despite their perceived power and wealth... mean and nasty people are usually suffering in ways that cannot be resolved with a mere million billion dollars.

I think I can finally accept the fact that people will always find a way to be mean and nasty. Regardless of their respective reasons for reaping rage in this world, I really do have a choice. And I choose NOT to take it personally. I choose life, love, and the true pursuit of happiness. I choose to refuse their nastiness... even if it's meant specifically and personally for me. I choose to:

_____

_____

_____

Give EVERYTHING Cheerfully

What do you have that is truly "yours?"

Besides your education (which is always a gift of your environment or someone else), what things are yours to keep forever? Is your jewelry yours? Is your automobile yours? Is your body yours?

Here's a thought (yours to keep if you want)…

As soon as we start the mental process of deciding what's mine and what's yours, we are soon doomed into a do-loop of deciding how best to protect, defend, and keep all **our** stuff.

Think about this: What if someone stole your car? How would you react? What if someone stole your watch, your wallet, or your winter coat in the middle of the coldest month? What would you do?

In *The Ideal* life, **you** give everything cheerfully.

Here's the Idea:
In order to give, you must first have "it" to give. If you have this, that, or the other, you are already tremendously blessed. Count your blessings.

Here's the Deal:
When you give what is yours, you will receive more than you ever thought possible. You get what you give. Give good or bad things; the choice is yours.

In building *The Ideal* world, I will...
Give Everything Cheerfully

Why do I think I need so much "stuff?" How much stuff is enough stuff? How much stuff do I have to acquire before I think I am living *The Ideal* life? If I had to make a list of 5 specific things that could, would, or should turn my life into *The Ideal* life, those 5 things are:

1. _____

_____

2. _____

_____

3. _____

_____

4. _____

_____

5. _____

_____

As much as I want the 5 things listed above, I also realize that I have so much more than I really need in my life. Accordingly, I will give these 2 things to someone who needs them much more than I do:

1. _____

2. _____

<u>FORGIVE</u>. Focus. Find.

What if someone stole your watch, your wallet, or your winter coat in the middle of the coldest month... what would you really do?

Worse yet, what if someone stole your heart? What if they smashed your dreams? What if they purposefully stole, smashed, or shattered your wonderful castle in the sky? What would you do?

Remember...
1) What if it *is* true?
2) What *can* you do about it?
3) What *will* you do about it?
4) What *are* you doing about it?

Regardless of the wrongs brought upon you, there is a very real power in giving an apology *before* it is given to you. Fore-give the apology. Give the apology, and you will lose the expectation to receive it. Give the apology, and you will lose all hate and discontent regarding the situation. Once you have truly forgiven others, you can focus on more important things in life. And, as you focus on positive things, you *will* achieve *The Ideal.*

Here's the Idea:
Once something is done, it's done. There is nothing you can do to change something that has already happened. Free yourself by freeing them.

Here's the Deal:
When you forgive, you release YOUR expectations.

**I know *The Ideal* world requires giving; I will...
*FORGIVE. Focus. Find.***

When I forgive, I set a prisoner free. And, ultimately, that prisoner will be me. If there were one magical phrase that could cure the world of all evil, shame, and shortsighted sin, it would be the simple phrase, "I forgive you."

I notice that the magical phrase is not the over-used, "I'm sorry" or "Please accept my apology." Fore-giving others an apology is not about blame. It's about accepting my imperfections by allowing the imperfections of others. I cannot change what has already happened. And if I remain angry or upset while waiting for an apology, I will never arrive at ***The Ideal*** life. However, if I give the apology to the offender before he gives it to me (if I *fore-give* the apology), the offender and the offense are no longer holding me back. Wow! I see how forgiveness can change my life - now!

I can finally accept: _____

_____

_____

My biggest challenge in this area is: _____

_____

_____

Here's what I **will** do: _____

_____

_____

Forgive. <u>FOCUS</u>. Find.

Obviously, you are reading these words. Thus, you are **focused** on the words of this page. If you have read the previous pages, you know and understand the **fact** that this one page does *not* define the entire message of this book

And like the pages in this book, today is only one page in the book of your life. The previous days help to place this day, today, into a broader context. Indeed, you were not born yesterday!

So as you go forward into the next pages of this book... and as you go forward into the next few days of your life, focus on the one item that matters more than any other thing in your life. Focus on today. Forget yesterday; it doesn't exist. Release tomorrow; you never had it anyway!

Most importantly, **focus** on what YOU *positively* want to achieve. Focus only on positive people, ideas, thoughts, activities, actions, and attitudes.

Here's the Idea:
It is literally impossible to think about two things at once. When you focus on today's positivity, you will begin to see more and more of today's possibilities.

Here's the Deal:
When you focus on the positive aspects of life, you will unconsciously overcome negativity and initiate events to achieve a profoundly positive life.

***The Ideal* world involves concentration; I will... Forgive. FOCUS. Find.**

What happens when I fore-give the apology? Does the offender "get away with" their offense? Why do *I* have to give the apology?

No matter what has happened in my life, I now understand that I cannot live in yesterday. *Giving an apology to someone when they should really apologize to me seems really odd.* However, I now see that forgiveness is really a form of acceptance.

When I forgive, I **accept** the fact that I cannot change what has already happened in my life.

After I give them the apology, I don't expect or need an apology from him or her; I can truly move on to other more important things in my life.

After I give them the apology, I will immediately begin to **adapt** to a life that no longer focuses on the unchangeable events of the past. In fact...

Now that I am not concerned about getting an apology, I can actually concentrate on things that really matter. I can actually focus on the only day that really exists: I can place my emphasis on today, and not the things that happened yesterday! After I accept and adapt (forgive), I can focus on what I really want to **achieve** in my life!

I can finally focus on my next three achievements:

1. _____

2. _____

3. _____

Forgive. Focus. <u>FIND.</u>

Take a quick moment and flip through the previous pages of this book. You have found the words and ideas on how to achieve **The Ideal** life. You have found a path to positive thinking. You have found a path to positive **action**. However, none of these words and ideas will work unless you start with one basic premise: Forgive.

Forgive yourself; forgive others; and move on. We have all made mistakes. No one is perfect. And no one in your life will ever be perfect. Yes, you will make many more mistakes in life. Yes, the person in the mirror will occasionally fumble the ball. Likewise, you should not expect other people to perform flawlessly at their mission in life. They, too, will make many more mistakes.

Plan to forgive people when they push your buttons. And now that you have the knowledge of this book, you know that **you are the only one pushing the buttons in the elevator of your life**.

When you truly forgive, you can faithfully focus on how to spend your time. You can find your true passion! Actually, your true passion will find you!

Here's the Idea:
As we seek The Ideal, disappointment may occur.

Here's the Deal:
As soon as you fore-give, you can focus and find freedom from the disappointments in life.

The Ideal life is right here, and I will...
Forgive. Focus. FIND.

I want to discover my true passions. I want to find my purpose for the life that I live. If I spend any amount of time looking backwards and hoping for an apology, I am wasting valuable time. On the other hand, if I continuously fore-give the apologies, I can actually focus on the gift of life that I have in today. I realize I am not perfect. In fact, no one in this entire world is perfect. And when I make my mistakes, I want to be forgiven... I want people to accept my apologies.

No matter what he or she has done to me...
As I turn the pages of this book, I have already fore-given the apology to him or her.

Now that I have freed them from my mental marker of mistakes, I, too, am free from the potential prison of perpetual pain and pity.

I am today. I am this moment. I am.

I now have the understanding and power of true forgiveness. I am now focused on *this* day. I now realize the fact that yesterday does not exist. Tomorrow is yet to be created. But today, this hour, this moment, this space in time is all mine.

Beginning today, I will find the meaning of my life:

_____

_____

_____

This *Will* Pass

What scares you the most?

Who makes you really, **really** angry?

What events bring out the worst in you?

What events bring out the absolute best in you?

Regardless of the scenario, just give it a minute, hour, or day... and it will pass. Interestingly, this mantra applies to good *and* the bad things in life.

For us to completely understand and appreciate the good stuff, we must have a firm appreciation of the bad stuff in life.

The driver that cuts you off will soon be long gone. Your super-important point that has to be made in the middle of a heated argument will fade with the setting sun. The worst grief in the world is rarely forgotten; but the worst of it will pass, and the rising sun will soon lift your spirit if you let it!

Here's the Idea:
Regardless of what happens this next second, today will move into tomorrow. This week will move into the next. And you will move beyond your current state of mind. The central question is... when will you CHOOSE to move on?

Here's the Deal:
Whatever "it" is... this, too, shall pass.

To arrive at *The Ideal* life, I must realize...
This WILL Pass

Everything passes. The biggest, oldest tree in the world will soon be gone. The tallest mountain will one day fall far below its current peak. I, too, will someday leave this earth.

As good as life is, the end will soon be here. As bad as life may seem, time is a gift of such great value. We must consistently remind ourselves of the rich depth and diversity that comes with reality.

Kahlil Gibran says it best in *The Prophet:*

Your joy is your sorrow unmasked. And the selfsame well from which your laughter rises was oftentimes filled with your tears. And how else can it be? The deeper that sorrow carves into your being, the more joy you can contain. Is not the cup that holds your wine the very cup that was burned in the potter's oven? And is not the lute that soothes your spirit, the very wood that was hollowed with knives? When you are joyous, look deep into your heart and you shall find it is only that which has given you sorrow that is giving you joy. When you are sorrowful look again in your heart, and you shall see that in truth you are weeping for that which has been your delight. Some of you say, "Joy is greater than sorrow," and others say, "Nay, sorrow is the greater." But I say unto you, they are inseparable. Together they come, and when one sits alone with you at your board, remember that the other is asleep upon your bed. You are suspended like scales between your sorrow and your joy. *

The Prophet (Gibran)

---

* *Kahlil Gibran, The Prophet (New York: Knopf, 2011) 29 – 30.*

Know Your Habits

What do you do every weekday, weekend, or Friday night? What foods do you enjoy "without even thinking about it?" For what television, radio, and other media do you make time? In everyday life, what are your specific habits?

All humans desire a certain level of consistency and uniformity. If you think you are the exception, ask yourself if you look forward to Friday, Saturday, December or July. Ask yourself, *"What would happen if the sun rose at 11AM instead of 6AM?"* As discussed in the chapter, *Priorities, Propensities, Presentations...* your habits drive your morning into the evening.

Habits are simply recurring actions that we subconsciously decide to do. Specifically:

hab·it *(noun)*:
  An established disposition of mind or character.

Habits are not necessarily bad or good. However, if you are not *aware* of your habits, you will never **change** your habits.

Here's the Idea:
Your character is developed by repetitive behavior.

Here's the Deal:
Changing habits is a life-changing event. Ready?

A cornerstone of *The Ideal* life is to...
Know Your Habits

What good habits do I really have? Dentists say I am supposed to brush and floss after every meal. Do I really brush my teeth after every meal? What other habits am I supposed to do... but, in reality, I have not been doing?

Perhaps more importantly, in what bad habits am I consistently investing my valuable time, energy, and effort? I am not a perfect person. Thus, I probably have a bad habit or three.

To be totally honest, I really need to change **five** habits in my life. Specifically, I need to:

1. _____

_____

2. _____

_____

3. _____

_____

4. _____

_____

5. _____

_____

Change Your Rituals

There is a huge difference between a habit and a...

> **rit·u·al** *(noun)*
>
> A detailed procedure regularly followed

A habit is an act or thought completed by the subconscious mind. Locking your door, tapping your finger on the desktop, and chewing on your lip or pencil are all examples of habits.

Rituals, on the other hand, are more likely to be driven by your *conscious* mind. Ritualistic events require us to invest thoughtful effort and preparation. Almost ceremonious in how we apply them, rituals are often symbolic of a greater ideal and are usually rooted in deep-seated beliefs.

Those deep-seated beliefs are often based on teachings from our early childhood or events we believe to be of great importance. Interestingly, rituals are merely choreographed, preparatory actions leading up to something of greater significance than the ritual. Elections, weddings, and, yes, funerals are ritualistic.

And believe it or not, starting your day can be ritualistic... **if** you invest the time and stop letting your habits get the best of your best day: today.

Here's the Deal:
> *Habits pave yester into day...*
> *Rituals make habits quickly go away.*

A bigger cornerstone of *The Ideal* life is to...
Change Your Rituals

From this day forward, I commit to investing at least a half- hour every day thinking about my habits and rituals. By investing a mere 30 minutes a day, I will begin to see my habits. However, some of my habits may be out of my viewpoint.

Accordingly, today I will listen to myself and study the subconscious choices I make (these are my habits). Today I will focus on the conscious set of actions I need to do (these are my rituals). I now realize that changing my rituals can be a life-changing experience. I *want* that experience!

What **three** habits/rituals negatively affect me?

1. _____

2. _____

3. _____
(Hint: Watching too much TV is a horrific habit)

What daily and weekly rituals do I take seriously?

_____

_____

What **three** rituals should I take more seriously?

1. _____

2. _____

3. _____

Awareness of Self

According to some historians, Al Capone, one of the most notorious mobsters in American history, truly believed he was doing a great service to the American people. Capone's gangsters murdered hundreds of people as the United States government implemented, and then repealed, *prohibition* (the sale of alcoholic beverages).

Like Al Capone, many people don't see or understand how nasty and mean they actually are. Many people are blinded by their own behavior. Many people reading the words on this page will never understand how important it is to achieve a high degree of self-awareness. Without the correct *awareness of self*, we will never see our *selves* for who we really are. Without awareness of self, we will remain locked in a delusional state of denial that will undermine everything we do.

However, when we strive to see our true *selves*, we will begin to uncover strengths and assets not previously visible to our singular senses.

Here's the Idea:
*To be aware is to be interested, alert, concerned, and informed. What do you <u>know</u> about **your** self?*

Here's the Deal:
Getting to know yourself is the first step toward changing your self. Getting to know yourself is potentially a life-changing event. Are you ready?

To achieve *The Ideal* life, we must gain...
Awareness of Self

Others may have an idea of what I am doing. But I am the only one who *knows* everything I do. No one else knows my thoughts. No one knows the extent of my spirituality, emotions, logic, or my finite limitations of self. Only I know these things.

However, as much as I **think** I **know** about me, there are things about me that are more easily seen by others. There are times when others may be more aware of my actions than I am. I may unknowingly offend someone. Or I might say something that is technically true, but socially unacceptable to say in a public forum. Yes... sometimes, only others see these things about me.

By becoming more aware of my SELF, I am better able to identify my strengths and weaknesses. Moreover, increasing knowledge of my SELF will help illuminate my good and bad behaviors. More importantly, I will see how these behaviors affect my attitude towards people, and my approach to how I can achieve **The Ideal** life. I now understand that enhanced self-awareness is essential for personal growth. From my point of view:

My top 2 strengths are:

1. _____

2. _____

My greatest fear is:

1. _____

2. _____

Alignment of Self

Who **are** you? What do you **really** believe?

Do your actions reflect your thoughts?

Do your thoughts reflect your innermost soul?

Regardless of the information contained in this (or any other) book, what **you** believe is true (to you). Regardless of how much knowledge you may have stored in your mind and heart, you will *use* only the knowledge you believe to be necessarily true.

Once you have achieved the correct **awareness** and **accurate belief** in your true self, you will soon have the knowledge of who you really are.   And for some of us, the Truth is a shocking revelation.

Do you really think about what you do? And do you really do what you think? Is there agreement between and among your mind, body, and soul?

Here's the Idea:
When discussing your "self" with your friends and family, there are at least three ways to view you: the way you see yourself; the way others see you; and the way you really are. Are they in agreement?

Here's the Deal:
*To achieve **The Ideal**, you must endeavor to become one with perception and reality.   This oneness is possible only by seeking Absolute Truth.*

Divided we fall; thus *The Ideal* life is based on...
Alignment of Self

Together we stand. Divided we fall.

Attributed to many orators over the past two hundred years, the above statement can be applied to a family, a business, a nation, and any other collective group of individuals and seemingly different entities. *It also applies to me.*

With proper alignment of my S.E.L.F., I can achieve almost anything I want to achieve. But what is this S.E.L.F.? And why does it need to be aligned?

Whether I believe it or not, I have four distinct parts of my SELF. They are:

S piritual

E motional

L ogical

F inite

Though many people will say the existence of my spirit can never be proved, I know *my* **s**pirit lives within *my* finite body. I also know my **e**motions are very important to me. And **l**ogically speaking, the things that others and I do in this world have to (logically) make sense to my **f**inite self.

These four attributes, when aligned with each other, form a powerful superhuman that is me. I want my super powers! And in Part 6 of *The Ideal*, I will find out exactly HOW to achieve my super powers! I want alignment of my SELF!

Your Guidance System

As you become more aware of your specific thoughts, actions, and the extensive, integrated connections between your thoughts and actions, you will clearly see the value in steering your thoughts toward only the best possible ideas.

By focusing on our best ideas, our actions will be drawn from a well that is filled with good, great, and gorgeous thoughts. Continuously drawing on the best thoughts will prevent us from making daytime and thought-space available for negative people, processes, and patterns of thought.

Continuously drawing on only our best thoughts allows us to align our true selves with an ideal.

But to what will you align your true self? What is the ONE THING on which you can depend? What is your guidance system?

Here's the Idea:
You control you. You alone are responsible and accountable for driving your self up and down this journey called life. Are you in or out of control?

Here's the Deal:
When you choose media to watch, listen to, and live by, you are literally choosing food for thought. When you choose food for thought, you must remember: You are what you eat. You must remember: You are choosing your guidance system.

What's Your Benchmark?

A benchmark is a scale used for measurement. Superbowl victories and academic grading systems are two examples of benchmarks. As a culture and country, we honor teams with multiple Superbowl victories. We also promote students when they achieve a certain standard of academic excellence in school. (A, A-, B+, B, etc.)

But whom do *you* honor with *your* attention? What leader of the kind, feeder of the mind, or seeder of the vine do you *pay* your attention? Moreover, do you imitate him, her, or them? Ask yourself, *"Who sets my standards? What is my idea of the best mother, greatest father, grandest granny, and best friend forever?"*

When gauging your own best behavior, to whom do you compare your greatest self? When feeling bad about what you did, to what standard do you fail to measure up? What is your benchmark?

Here's the Idea:
There is often a subtle comparison between where you are and where you think you could or should be.

Here's the Deal:
By starting a series of focused rituals, you can establish an entirely new set of standards to strive toward. When you accept your new standards, you will adapt to a new way of thinking, acting, and interacting. You will literally create a new you.

***The Ideal* life is created and maintained by...**
Your Guidance System and Benchmarks

Who told me vegetables are good for me?

How do I *know* gravity and tall buildings can cause serious damage to the human body?

Somewhere along my path in life, I was provided a signpost or two. During my deepest dejections, I found something, someone, somehow to get me through my valley. Likewise, someone somehow was there to guide me to my highest highs.

As I move forward and toward ***The Ideal*** life, I need to stop right here on this path... my path. I need to take one small step back and look around at many of the other paths already discovered by the great men and women of history.

Though my path is mine alone, there are so many lessons to be learned from those who have been kind enough to share knowledge of their mistakes.

Indeed: *"If I only knew then what I know now..."* Well, now's my chance to take that phrase to a whole new level. I have the opportunity to take a long, hard look at my guidance system.

I need to place my values, thoughts, and dreams under a personal microscope and see how I arrived at my current guiding values, beliefs, and principles. What have I carried with me since childhood? It's time to invest serious thought into the fundamental concepts, beliefs, and philosophies that make up my guidance system.

*Who & what has helped to create the magic of **me**?*

Part 4: Your Next Steps:

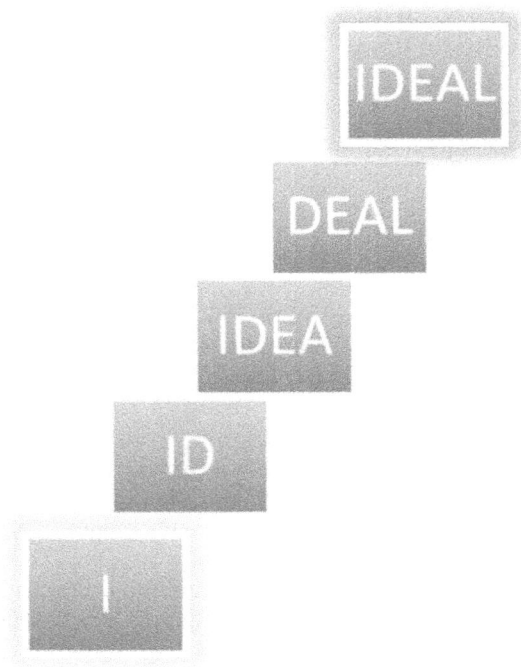

Two Distinct Options

Every single step of life begins with a conscious decision to step forward (or backward); left (or right); up (or down). This way or that way?

And since every journey starts with one small step, every single journey begins with a conscious decision to step "somewhere."

Sometimes we step in the same spot, over and over again. We "mark time" and "mock time" by repeatedly stepping into the same tracks. However, time is not to be mocked. In fact, time cannot be mocked. *"Time" does not even exist.*

Oh, sure… we can try to measure the seconds, minutes, hours, and years between one event and another. But those are mere units of time… units of absolutely nothing. Yet… paradoxically, time is everything. Time is all we ever really have.

The question is: What, exactly, are you doing with your time? More specifically, what option are you selecting? Left or right? Backward or Forward?

Here's the Idea:
Life is a journey. What are you walking to & from?

Here's the Deal:
Every decision is a step toward one thing… and two steps away from something else. Choose wisely.

The Ideal life is based on the fact that I have...
Two Options

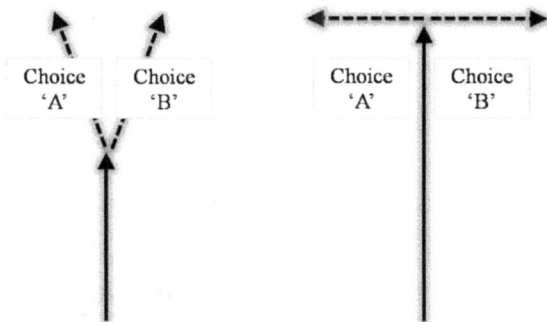

Choice 'A'   Choice 'B'   Choice 'A'   Choice 'B'

Choices are to be compared to a 'T' and not a 'Y'.

I see that there is no proverbial fork in the road.

When choosing between two distinct choices, there may appear to be similar characteristics among the available choices. However, in reality, my two available choices are *directly* opposite each other. In my quest for **The Ideal** life, I must seriously consider and understand the fact that my decisions to choose this over that may have simple-but-significant effects on the next five minutes, the next five days, or the next five years.

Today, I choose to *stop* doing **ONE** thing, and it is:

_____

Today, I choose to *start* doing **ONE** thing, and it is:

_____

The Elevator of Life

POSITIVE

Have you ever heard the expression, *"Think outside the box?"* Ironically, in today's boxed-in world, *thinking outside the box* is almost impossible. We sleep on a box. We shower in a box. We live in a box. We drive in a box. We work in a box. Most of our external thinking is done in a box (computer). And we often get our (fast) food in a box. Yes: our lives are full of boxes.

But the most important box is the elevator.

Like the elevator in buildings, *The Elevator of Life* starts with one simple choice. As we stand before the closed doors of the yet-to-be-called elevator, we have one decision to make: ***Up or down?***

We awake in the morning and set a course for an office building, service job, or manufacturing facility. And though we don't spend much time thinking about ***how*** we will get there, we usually arrive at the correct address; we select an appropriate floor of the proper building; and then arrive at our office or workstation destination.

Likewise, *The Elevator of Life* offers an opportunity to *choose the direction of our attitude* every hour of the day. And if we can set a course for one full day of positive thought and action, we can probably put together two days of the same.

Which button will you press: Up or down?

If you press the 'up' button, the elevator will take you up.   If you press the 'down' button, the elevator will certainly take you down.   And in our respective lives, selecting a good or bad attitude is as simple as pushing a button.

However, on too many occasions, we blame others for our attitude. We blame coworkers or spouses for making us mad. We blame children for making us lose our temper. We blame our jobs for making us unhappy. We blame, we blame, and we blame.

Why do we freely give so much blame to others?

Instead of giving the blame to others, let's accept our response-able roles in pressing the single button that raises or lowers *The Elevator of Life.*

In a real elevator, when you get off at the wrong floor, you don't blame other people!

You don't blame other people if you push the *down* button when you actually wanted to go up to a higher floor!

Accordingly, don't blame other people when your personal attitude is in a downward spiral.

Perhaps *The Elevator of Life* seems too simplistic.

Or perhaps you think it doesn't apply to daily life or how you think. Well, consider what happens once you walk into the elevator in a building. You are faced with another choice: To what floor will you travel? Is your yet-to-be-chosen floor above or below your present location? *Up or down?*

Likewise, in *The Elevator of Life*, regardless of how you arrived at your current place in life, you have one simple choice to make: To what location will you go from here? *Up or down?*

Where you currently stand is important.
Where you are going is <u>MORE</u> important!

Everyone faces challenges. Some challenges appear insurmountable and hopeless. However, as you stand in your respective box, you are faced with one critical choice: Will your thoughts and actions descend downward into the deep, darkest pit of despair? Or will you press the *up* button and self-exalt yourself out of your current malaise?

By actively, consistently, and persistently choosing to push the *up* button, your *Elevator of Life* will escalate higher. And as sailors and pilots everywhere know, *height of eye* determines your ability to see **over** the horizon. The higher your **altitude**, the farther you can see past the current horizon. Likewise, the higher your **attitude**, the better you can see past your current problems.

And as your height of attitude grows, so, too, will your ability to forgive others, focus on the positive, and find your mission in life. As you accept, adapt, and achieve... you will soon live, think, and play far outside of the box. You will achieve **The Ideal.**

Here's the Idea:
It is impossible to think about two things at once. When we focus on positivity, we see more positivity.

Here's the Deal:
Focus on the positive aspects of life, and you will automatically overcome negativity.

In *The Ideal* life, we all face the same allegory... *The Elevator of Life*

Sure, I could look back at any particular episode in my life and figure out a way to blame this, that, or the other for my situation.

But that's like getting off the elevator and staying stuck on the "wrong floor." In reality, there is no "wrong floor." As long as I am alive and reading the pages of this book, I have a very credible opportunity to do something great with my life. What is this *great* thing I can do with my life?

I can simply live it!

And I can live it to the fullest.

I will not allow lessons to be seen as mistakes.

I will not get stuck on the *wrong floor.*

Every floor I have ever walked has added some form of value to my life. Best of all, I now realize that I can simply and literally turn myself and my attitude around, face the elevator door once again... and push the *up* button. Yes, it is true: My attitude determines my altitude. And today, I want *The Ideal* life.

Today, I accept the fact that, regardless of what has happened in the previous days of my life, I still retain the awesome power to choose my attitude. No one else has this power to change me. **Only me.**

I can *always* push the up button!

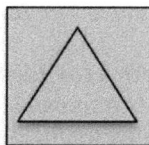

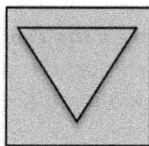

One simple superlative

su·per·la·tive *(noun)*
1. A thing that excels all others; a highest quality.
2. The highest degree; peak.

So... in the simplest of terms, these are the facts:

To achieve *The Ideal*,

1) You have to accept the fact that you are response-able for your life.

2) You must adapt to the constantly changing conditions in your life.

3) You must achieve a state of forgiveness.

Like the elevators of the physical world, you alone choose the direction of your life. Regardless of what "they" do to you (your boss, your spouse, your mate, your child, your parent, your dog, your cat, or your favorite politician), you alone choose the direction of your life.

You choose your own superlatives. You choose your guidance systems and your benchmarks. You choose who, what, where, when, and why you do what you do.

But what is a "good" superlative? What is the one thing that can immediately change your life forever? What superlative do I recommend to change your life? In a word, the only thing that can change your life is YOU. Indeed, other things can help, but when it comes to who, what, where, when, and why... it is YOU that matters most.

Who, What, Where, When, and Why?

Who?

Who is the most important person in the world?

~ You ~

For whom is this little book of advice made? You.

Who can bring you the worst sadness? Only you.

Who interacts with everyone you know? You.

Who can give you the best happiness? You.

Who is really in charge of your life? You.

Who is the only person who can forgive all the bad things that have ever happened to you? Only you.

Who is the only person who can focus all of your energy and efforts toward *The Ideal* life? You.

Who is the only person who can find your specific mission? Among the million billion things to do on this great planet called Earth, who is the only person who can truly change the way you think?

~ You ~

You are the only person in the whole world who can decide what you will do, where and when you will do it, and why you will choose one person, place, or thing over many other people, places, and things. When it comes to changing you…

*You are the most powerful person in **your** world.*

What?

What do you really want to do with your life?

A more specific question is *"What do you want to do with the remaining years, months, weeks, days, and minutes of your life?"* [Tick tock, tick tock]

As stated earlier in the preceding chapter *Traditions and Transitions*, "your grandest beauty is when you are in the midst of transition."

And get this:

You are always in the midst of transition!

The question is:

To what condition are you currently headed?

As you continue to read the second half of this little book, ask yourself if you are ready to apply the knowledge you have gained from reading a quick course on how to achieve *The Ideal* life.

More importantly, remind yourself of "what" we are discussing within these few pages.

We are not discussing some philosophical theory.

We are not discussing your past challenges.

We are discussing your **current** life - today.

We are discussing your **remaining** years.

We are discussing your **ideal** life.

Where?

When someone mentions the word *where*, we tend to think of a geographic location.

"Where did you get that book?"

"Where did you get that dress; that car; that tie?"

For the purpose of achieving **The Ideal** life, take a moment, pause from reading this book, lift your eyes from the words on this page, and look around the area in which you are sitting or standing.

In what building, city, state, or country are you?

Where are you? How did you get **here**?

Indeed, some time ago, you travelled to your current location. At some point in the past, you made a conscious decision to move from where you were... and to stop and be where you **are**.

Similarly, where **are** you in the midst of your life?

Are you focused on the best thoughts and ideas?

Or are you waiting for a magic cure?

If you are looking for a magic cure, look in the mirror. Look deep into the soul of that one person staring back at you. Those eyes lead to the soul that will prep your thoughts, clear your mind, and pave your path to **The Ideal** life.

Let's move from where you currently are...

When?

Say this one word aloud:

Click!

There... you have now flipped the switch and made the move toward **The Ideal** life. You are now armed with very real knowledge, and you are fully prepared to live a life of wisdom. Literally speaking, your mind has already been changed by the words of this book. You have been educated on the best way to find true happiness. *(Give happiness, and you will **find** it where you give it).*

You have been introduced to the simple ideas and simpler deals on how to achieve **The Ideal**.

Through the previous pages, you have been advised to stop paying attention to certain things. And you have been counseled to start paying attention to your habits, rituals, and your self.

Perhaps you have read or heard this powerful advice once, twice, or a hundred times before.

Or maybe these concepts are entirely new to you.

In either case, you have already taken the biggest step required to effect immediate and lasting change: You have accepted the simple knowledge herein. Moreover, you are already adapting to your newfound knowledge.

When did you make this great, grand change?

You made this great, grand change today.

Why?

Why is change necessary? Why is your "old" life not good enough? Actually, you only have one life.

And your one life is only one thread in an interdependently woven quilt of a million billion other threads constantly moving, changing, and rearranging things throughout the world.

And as your world changes, you must also change.

In reality, you are not the same *type* of person you were yesterday. Indeed, you are the same *person*; but you have since seen a newer version of the world. You have thought different thoughts. And, yes, you have already changed into a newer version of your previously existing self.

Your changes from yesterday are seemingly small. However, yesterday something happened that has forever changed who you are. Something happened yesterday that will affect today, tomorrow, and every day hereafter.

What happened? **You** happened. You represent the very nature of change. You are yesterday; you are today. And, yes... going forward, you are the culmination of years of choices, chores, and challenges; days of decisions, dreams, and drama; minutes of mental mayhem; and seconds of significant stuff shaping the very life that is you.

So the question is not "*Why* should you change?"

The question is...
> **How** *can you make change work for you?*

Part 5: HOW to Get There

Above everything, your perspective matters most.

Accordingly, as you begin this path to real change, start by studying what you believe to be true.

Remember:
*Believing is one thing; **knowing** is everything.*

Moreover, how much knowledge of your true self do you really have? What do you believe about yourself?   What do you know about yourself? Often, the things that people think and believe about themselves are quite different than what they know about themselves.

To put it another way: In many cases, you already know what you need to work on; you just haven't started the work yet.

However, despite what you may **think** *you know* about yourself, there are probably hundreds, if not thousands of things you simply don't see. And, if you don't see the behaviors, you are not likely to change the behaviors.

Accept this fact:

Your roadmap to change must start with your acceptance of the fact that your priorities and habits, regardless of how good or bad they may seem, are often far outside of your point of view.

Don't just believe this. Know it!

The Clark Model of Life Leadership

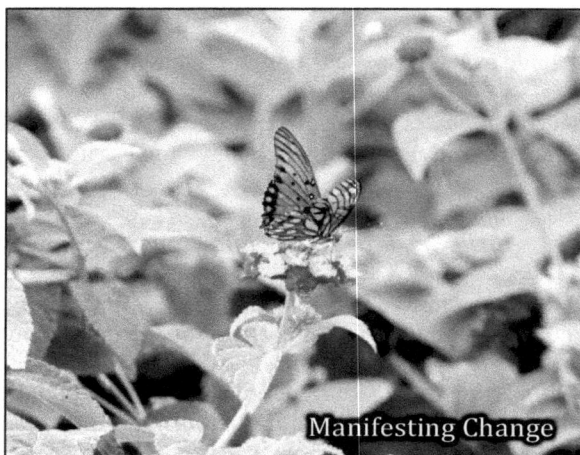

Manifesting Change

The previous chapters of this book are focused on helping you accept one very important fact about your specific life: **Your** *perspective matters most.*

Regardless of whether or not your beliefs are based on fact or fiction, your perspective matters more than anything else in this world.

This section of **The Ideal** is provided to help you see and understand **how** your perspective dominates your priorities and your propensity to do certain things.

This section is an explanation of *The Clark Model of Life Leadership* – a simple, account of how we see our life, prioritize our life, and let our *old* life continue to control our current life.

The Clark Model of Life Leadership consists of

- **Presentations**
- **Priorities**
- **Propensities**
- **The Loop**

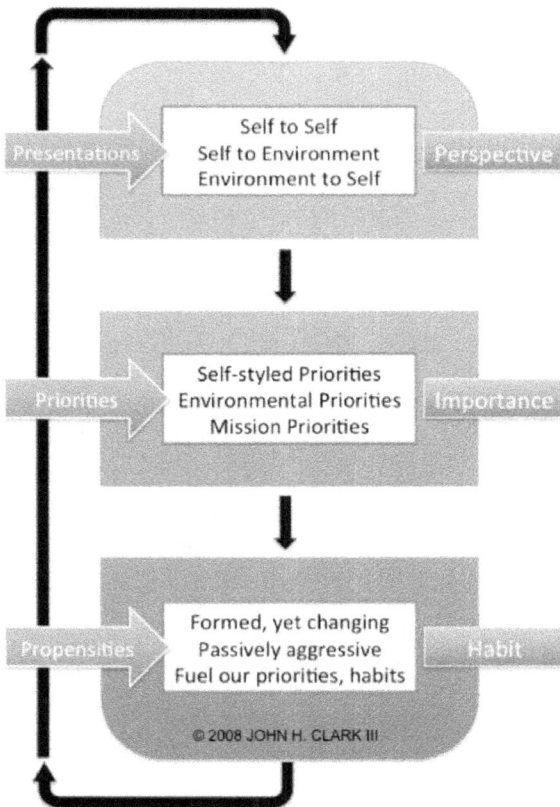

The Clark Model of Life Leadership

	Self to Self	
Presentations	Self to Environment	Perspective
	Environment to Self	

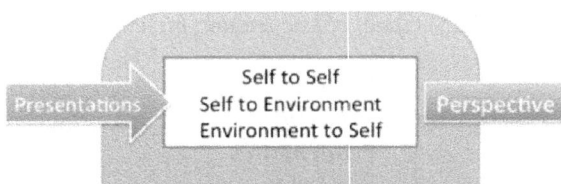

Presentations. Often referred to as perspectives, presentations are the physical, mental, and social lenses of your True Self. More than mere perspectives, presentations are indicative of how you present things to others and to yourself.

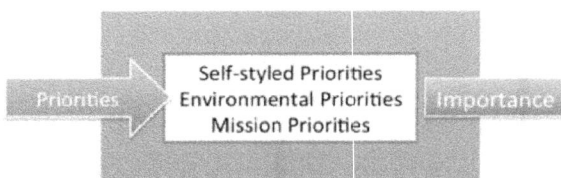

	Self-styled Priorities	
Priorities	Environmental Priorities	Importance
	Mission Priorities	

Priorities. From the time you wake up, you prioritize our day. You prioritize the order of making breakfast and getting dressed. And you prioritize the status of friends, family, and foe.

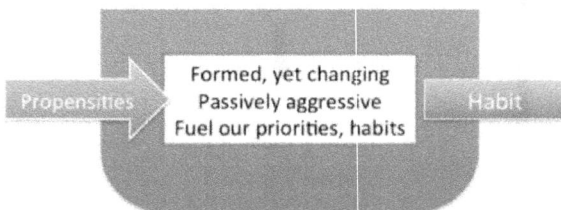

	Formed, yet changing	
Propensities	Passively aggressive	Habit
	Fuel our priorities, habits	

Propensities. These are the habits and routines that keep you on your current path. Interestingly, your daily habits actually work to *prevent* you from changing your highly patterned life. Your propensities are already formed, but they are also dynamic, and subject to change at any time.

DEAL

The Loop. The fourth component of *The Clark Model of Life Leadership* is The Loop. It connects each component to the other two components. And it affects each component in the exact same way: ***It strengthens and perpetuates the status quo. It is the deal you make with your thoughts, your actions, and your environment.***

The Loop keeps you where you are.

The Loop prevents change. *The Loop* fuels denial. *The Loop*, though having no real power or separate and distinct characteristic, keeps your habits fueling other habits. And it keeps your priorities arranged "just so."

Without *The Loop*, our presentations, priorities, and propensities are mutually exclusive and independent.

However, with *The Loop*, each feature is inextricably bound to the other two characteristics. With *The Loop*, there is an undeniable connection between what we see (or don't see), how we arrange our lives, and what we tend to do.

Ironically, *The Loop* is both a barrier and an access to real, immediate, and permanent change.

But how is this possible?

How can *The Loop* be so damning, and yet so redeeming? How can the same integrating link help us disintegrate the same characteristics it so strongly links?

The answer is in the shortcut we often take. Specifically:

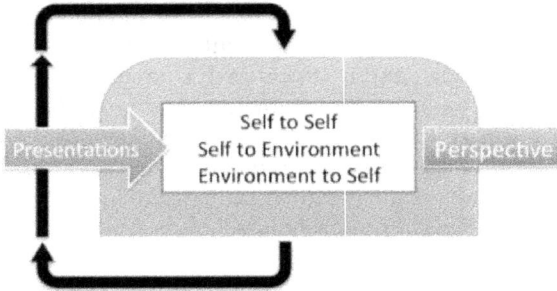

Study the altered version of *The Clark Model of Life Leadership* above. Notice how *The Loop* has been changed to feed directly back into the presentations. Without the proper perspective and **presentation to self,** we will never have an accurate view of our priorities or propensities. And without an accurate view of those two aspects, we remain unable to effect real change in our lives. *We cannot change what we cannot see.*

*Accordingly, focus on how you **view** the world.*

Instead of focusing on pesky priorities and hellacious habits, focus your energy on changing your presentations. When you change your presentations, you can actually **see** how your priorities may need to change. When you change your presentations, your thoughts, habits and propensities will *automatically* begin to change.

IDEA This discussion on propensities and habits may seem common sense or perhaps somewhat obvious. However, *The Clark Model of Life Leadership* exemplifies the extent to which our integrated humanistic characteristics are resistant to change. In other words...

Changing priorities may be relatively easy.

But changing habits is not as easy.

Changing presentations is even more difficult.

Changing all three at one time is an amazingly difficult task. But why is this task so challenging?

Breaking the loop requires strength greater than yours. Breaking the loop requires superhuman strength to re-create a whole new sense of self.

Breaking the loop requires one superhuman act. By choosing to complete this one simple act, you will change your life in ways that are currently unimaginable. You will change how you perpetuate and prioritize your world.

Change your perspective.

Seeing is Believing

ID

People have often described life as a *race*. Perhaps it is. And in the end, the race is long, but only with your self.

Presentations are viewpoints that dominate everything else. You present yourself to yourself; you present your self to the world (environment); and you present the world to yourself (via preconceived notions and through your previously lived and learned life experiences).

Presentations are the common elements that bring the mission and the environment into one place (interdependence). If you can accept reality for what it is, and if you can objectively consider (but reject) *unrealistic* points of view, you can begin to work from a position of Truth, and deny the **Id** its greedy need for immediate gratification.

However, if you continue to see, seek, and support a perspective that is different than a Truth-based reality, your efforts at change are based on a lie. And everything based on a fabrication is a mere manifestation of that same fabrication. Everything based on a lie will soon logically falter. Buildings, bridges, and lives built on faulty foundations will someday fall. Thus, to avoid future tragedy, absolute Truth should be your yardstick, your benchmark, and your best measure of success.

The environment changes when you enter into it. Everywhere you go... **You change the world.**

Your Sixth Sense

But whose world is it? When does **the** world become **your** world? When is your environment more important than your self? When is the mission paramount? When should you relegate your self to the back burner?

The best way to ask and honestly answer these questions is to accurately assess the current environment of which you are a part. And the only way to accurately assess anything is to receive and recognize stimuli through our six available senses:

1. Seeing
2. Touching
3. Hearing
4. Tasting
5. Smelling
6. **Perceiving**

It is the 6th sense of *perceiving* that we must learn to strengthen. For the most part, self, society, and shame have weakened our 6th sense. Our physical, finite self is in constant conflict with our perceiving, intuitive, spiritual self. Over time, our perceptions (*and presentations to self*) become blurred by the input from media, television, friends, family, enemies, and to a certain extent, our very physical feelings about our self.

As a matter of fact, people tend to view their propensities and priorities through their own ***flawed presentations***. Many people are oblivious to their very own horrible habits and ridiculous priorities. In an ironic twist of reality, it is our very own perspective of the world that prevents us from seeing what we absolutely ***need*** to see.

And until we learn to correctly see our presentations (of self, environment, and mission), there is a distinct possibility (and a probability) that we may never see what we absolutely need to see. Until we learn to subscribe to a more authoritative perspective of ourselves, we will remain in the same situational funk, regardless of the various remedies we may try.

Right now, to effect true positive change, you need to agree that your view of your environment is, ironically, **constrained** by your view of the environment. Moreover, your perception of the environment is most likely considerably different than the actual circumstances occurring within the environment. Up until now, you probably have not even considered how dramatically the environment changes when you enter into it.

Yes, our first 5 senses educate us about the world.

Through sight, we can distinguish the expectations of a raincloud on the horizon. And we can see a car rapidly approaching the next intersection.

Through touch, we can experience the tenderness of a hug and the prickliness of a rosebush.

Through hearing, we can be entertained by melodious music, and we can also be startled by unexpected sounds.

Through taste, we can tell whether the chicken is spicy or sweet, and we can enjoy an after-dinner dessert.

Through smell, we know when the cake is baked, and we also know when the cake has baked a little too long.

But it is your sixth sense that truly governs your life. It is your presentation of the world to yourself, your perspective, that rules, governs, and guides your propensities and priorities. And once you change your presentations, you will begin to change everything else... *everything*.

You may not think of your current priorities as wrong, wretched, or requiring significant tweaking. For the most part, people believe their current priorities are great *(primarily because many people don't fully see or compare their existing priorities with a True benchmark)*.

Likewise, you may not believe your habits are affecting other areas of your life... simply because you literally don't see how your propensities are influencing your self in all areas of your *life (not just the areas of life you can readily identify)*.

You may have heard the phrase "the blind leading the blind." Well, in your own personal mission of life leadership, the very same thing can happen to you. In areas where you are blind, you simply cannot lead. Well, perhaps you *can* lead, but without guidance, the results might be disastrous.

Like the military commander who is clueless in battlefield leadership, if you are clueless in the skills required to navigate through the hazards of life, you and others in your life will soon face some rather tragic life-leadership-related consequences. If a military leader is blind to the traps, trips, and trickery of the enemy, how can he be expected to successfully lead the troops to success? If you are blind to your own traps, trips, and trickery of self-inflicted denial, how can you be expected to successfully lead yourself through the *Valley of the Shadow of Death?*

Accordingly, let's continue an analysis of *The Clark Model of Life Leadership* by accepting and understanding your greatest personal limitations. You may have an awesome set of priorities. And maybe you have superb well-thought-out habits.

But if your view of the world is slightly (or greatly) shaded by preconceived negative notions, beliefs, or teachings, success will always be a relative, moving target. Saddam Hussein was an accomplished head of state, as was Adolph Hitler. These were men of great evil power and irrational influence. Perhaps their rise to power can be attributed to their habitual need for power. Or maybe their irrational influence was gained through a lifetime of placing power at the top of their priority list. Regardless of their path to power, they truly believed and perceived that their view of the world was an accurate view.

These men may represent extreme examples of how badly the human perspective can go wrong. However, the passengers on the *Titanic* were equally wrong in their perceptions. Teenagers are equally wrong about their invulnerabilities. And many adults are similarly wrong in the estimation of their ability to see things for how they are... especially items related to self.

Take a look at *The Clark Model of Life Leadership* on the next page. You can readily see how propensities and priorities are previewed, viewed, and reviewed and looped through presentations. Unfortunately, propensities and priorities are more likely to be overlooked as they pass through the presentations. This overlooking is, in effect, a naturally strong form of denial. Unfortunately, the stronger the denial, the more blind we become.

Remember: If your view of the world is obstructed, colored, or shaded by *anything* (beliefs, teachings, etc.), then success will always be a relative, moving target.

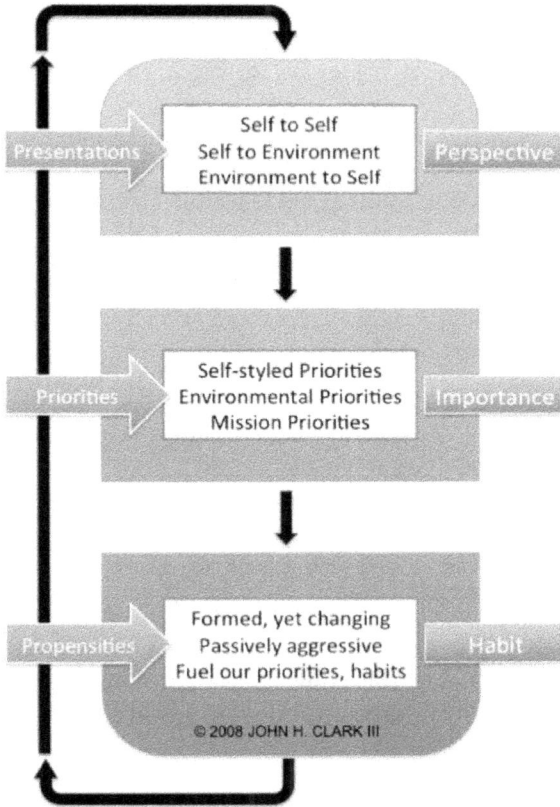

The Clark Model of Life Leadership

Moreover, in a horrific loop of ludicrousness, the more blind we become, the deeper our denial digs us into ditches of doubt, danger, and damage.

To effect true change, you must start with a fresh view of the world. You must shift your current perspective from *your way* to *a different way* of seeing the world. You already have a point of view... a perspective... a manner in which you present the world to yourself. Your current point of view, your existing perspective, and the current, existing *presentations to self* should be shattered and then re-created... but from a different perspective -- a different *presentation* of self.

CHANGE YOUR VIEW... CHANGE YOUR WORLD

Many people don't understand the filters affecting their specific view of the world. People often don't understand how their personal actions affect how they present themselves to the world. In fact, many people simply don't comprehend that they, themselves, control their filters, their actions, and their very own world *(reactions to their actions)*.

Without self and *the study of self* therein, what is there? Without adequate development of the inner (and outer) being, the other elements of environment and mission are totally disassociated... landscape without throughput, and paint without canvas. Without the captain, there is only the ship tossed upon the waves. Without you, there is only the environment and "stuff" to get done. In the final analysis, you are the most important aspect of this conversation.

Most importantly, in the context of presentations, great life leadership requires significant effort toward an ultimate alignment of *presentation* of self to self; *presentation* of self to environment; and *presentation* of environment to self.

These terms may seem confusing. To review, keep in mind the three dynamic (changing) parts of your world:

1. How you *see* yourself
   - Self to self
2. How you *present* yourself to the world
   - Self to environment
3. How you *see* the world
   - Environment to self

When all three facets of presentation are of the same accord, *then* you have the basis for being a great life leader. When you achieve this rare feat, *then* you will understand the vast array of information that is comprised of you and your environment... and integrated into your true self.

Only then will you be able to surmise the difference between **perception** and **reality**. *Then* you can understand which characteristics affect, promote, and deter real change in your true self.

Finally, once you accept and understand the relative importance of your presentations, you can spend more time addressing and changing your perspective... and less time on your priorities and propensities. **Seeing is believing !**

When you change your perspective...
Your propensities *automatically* change.

Part 6: Your Ideal Roadmap

Know this:

**A bend in the road is not the end of the road
unless YOU fail to make the turn!**

The previous pages of this book have expressed who, what, where, when, and why you must align your thoughts to a specific pattern of priorities, propensities, & presentations. You are now ready to apply specific steps to achieve *The Ideal* life.

Turn the page to start the next best chapter in the great life called YOU. Turn the page and discover **how** to navigate your journey along an unknown road in *The Ideal* life. For this journey, you are hereby provided eleven milestones to literally change your life. These **11 Ideals** are your keys to ensuring you are the best life leader for your life.

∽**1**∽

Obtain Awareness of Self

As you read through the previous pages of this book, you made a deliberate choice to seek a world where "happiness" is more than a passing state of being. You have read about traditions, transitions, priorities, propensities, and presentations. You have been educated on the allegorical, yet very real, *Elevator of Life*. And hopefully you have grasped more than a passing glimpse of the loving life that can be lived if you follow a few simple but powerful practices.

Hopefully, you are sincerely interested in moving past the mere **ownership** of information into the rich realm and realistically based world of the **application** of knowledge.

The *application of knowledge* is the definition of *being wise*. Remember: You can be the most educated person in the world. But if you don't use your knowledge, you are knowledgably ignorant.

The previous pages of this book provide the knowledge of who, what, where, when, and why you must align your thoughts to a specific pattern of priorities, propensities, and presentations. This knowledge is literally (now) **in** you; it is now a part of the living, breathing person that is you.

The previous pages of this book provide a concise, compact collection and expert education of acute, accurate awareness attributes. You have walked a path that most people will never seek nor find.

You now have a new awareness.

You have a new awareness about life, love, and living a life of love. You have **know**ledge of the concept of awareness. Your awareness can now serve as a foundation for discovering the four integrated aspects of your SELF...

Spiritual, Emotional, Logical, Finite

Please note the term *SELF*. Throughout the remainder of *The Ideal*, you will see the acronym/word *SELF*. This acronym denotes four separate areas of every living human being. It is important to understand and **know** that every person on the planet has these exact same parts of self. Below is a quick look at these aspects of the human existence, and how each relates to life.

Spiritual: Without getting into religious overtones and supernatural implications, the human spirit is simply the part of us that is uniquely associated with our physical flesh, yet unrestrained, if not unrelated to the other three forms of SELF.

Emotional: Though many theories exist on the exact cause of emotions, in general, Emotional *SELF* is that part of our thought process that is driven by, (and also affects) the biochemical and externally associative events in our life.

Logical: For the purpose of achieving *The Ideal* life, Logical *SELF* is comprised of our innate and learned ability to rationally and realistically infer and imply cause, effect, and some form of truth.

Finite: There is a limit to what we can do. Our bodies represent the physical and limited aspects of the *SELF*. Our bodies need food and shelter. If we don't get what we need, we will perish. Likewise, there are other limits to what we can do.

Your next step is to see, believe, and know how an increased **knowledge of your SELF** begins with an awareness of these four distinct yet integrated and influential parts of the person that is you. It is important that you not only learn about these unique parts of yourself, but also become aware of the significant interdependence each part shares with the other three parts of yourself.

In other words, though the parts are distinct and totally different from each other, without the other aspects present, the individual parts won't survive in your individualistic existence. Your **F**inite *SELF* might live on life support systems long after your brain has suffered a severe injury; but will your **L**ogical or **E**motional *SELF* remain intact?

More importantly...

Which of the four aspects of *SELF* has the greatest impact on you? Which of the four are you most inclined to change immediately. Which of the four aspects might require significant time, energy, and effort to change within the individual that is you?

For the purposes of this book, it is not necessarily important for you to become an expert on how to optimize all four areas of your *SELF.* However, it is **very** important for you to consider the impact of being significantly strong in one area, yet dangerously weak in any of the other three areas.

Think of your *SELF* as a four-legged table upon which you are literally building your life. As you go forward in life, you may want to consider paying attention to four supremely important legs:

Spiritual, Emotional, Logical, Finite.

Discover your true SELF.

What do you really reflect in the world?

S piritual

E motional

L ogical

F inite

∼2∼

Accept a Few Truths About Life

For the most part, we all want the same things.

There is only one magic formula...
But no one seems to know that formula.

Yes... If it doesn't kill you,
it will probably make you stronger.

*Forgiveness really **does** work.*

Money can cause as many problems as it solves.

Your life is measured in time... NOW!
Reality television is not your reality.

There is a time for doing it fast, doing it slow,
and perhaps, not doing it at all.

I am the most unique person in the world
... and so are you.

I am not perfect... and neither are you
(or anyone else).

Some people will never appreciate you.
Get over it.

Sooner or later... You will die.

When you appreciate something...
It appreciates in value.

Today, you are alive. Appreciate Life.
Live.

We all want the same things in life.

We all seek the same sense of self.

We all need the same assurance.

We fish... we find... we feed.

∼3∼

Accept and Adapt to Reality

Jumping from awareness to acceptance may seem like a rather large leap. You may be wondering how these terms relate, and how they form the basis for your personal roadmap to **The Ideal** life.

Awareness implies a certain wakefulness and mindfulness. Reading this book provides a basis for a newfound awareness and strengthened spirit. This collective knowledge is a tool to move you beyond a state of ignorance regarding what really "is." When you accept reality for what it is, your innermost self begins to change into a life-force of *solution* and a source of *synergy*. Unlike the people who choose to remain in the depths of denial and despair, you and this newfound ability to accept reality can drive your subconscious mind to a subliminal synchronicity with several sources of strength that can assist in solving the most complex issues with the simplest solutions.

Many people fail to understand the futility of denial (which is the opposite of acceptance). Unfortunately, when people refuse to accept reality, they create an alternate existence that is based on a lie. And though the alternate existence may appear to grow soundly, solidly, and in a superior fashion, the faulty foundation of denial will ensnare and ensure a spectacular demise of the storied creation that has been built on that lie.

But today, your awareness and understanding of the power of acceptance is the foundation for your next step. You are now capable, qualified, and enthusiastically encouraged to begin adapting.

Your qualifications will not protect you from attacks. This world is filled with a diverse population of people who are sure to help you smile, swear, and see red from time to time.

But because you have acquired a certain sense of awareness of self, spirit, and simple but sensationalized "supernatural" states of nature, you already know that life will require some degree of change. In other words, sooner or later, you will have to adapt to changing situations, stipulations, circumstances, and happenstances.

However, if you *really* want to achieve a powerful sense of synergistic, superhuman strength... use the combination of your acute **awareness** and your ability to **accept** reality. Openly engage the very real challenges in life by first receiving the reality of the situation as a "Capital 'T' Truth."

Warning: Here is an important caveat:
Never underestimate the power of denial.

Death, divorce, deadly combat, and dumb decisions, along with many other sorts of destruction are often buried in some dark corner of our mind... simply because we don't want to embrace the reality of the Capital 'T' Truth.

Refusal to embrace the reality does not remove, renounce, or rescind that reality. The best we can do (and we should always do our best)... is to seek awareness, accept the reality, and then adapt to that situation according to the strength of spirit that each of us has in each other and ourselves.

Yes... we are much stronger when we link.

And you know so much more than you think.

Sooner or later...

You *will* adapt to changing situations,

stipulations, circumstances,

and happenstances.

Chart your new course today !

~**4**~

Set Goals. Make Plans. Achieve Dreams.

Okay... here's the deal: You simply cannot go backwards. So stop right here and right now, and tell me: What do you want to do? State it now!

The micro-chapters of this book are designed to give you a crash course in several specific Absolute Truths. **Remember**: Your belief system dictates how you live your life. Quite simply, **you** choose what **you** want to believe. Accordingly, this little book of knowledge has presented the world "as it is." In reality, denial is a very capable and corrupt enemy. Denial is rich in resources, and it will use every ounce of your self.

Regardless of what I say in this book, you are the most powerful person in your world. You are the one who must focus on the words of this book. *The Ideal* is a formula for achieving a clear picture of potential ideas, from which you can then make the best possible deal with your thoughts and reality. *Your* formula starts with a profound statement of what you want to do. Do *not* state what you do *not* want to do. Don't waste your time, energy, and effort thinking about the things you don't want. Focus on what you want to do.

What do you want? What do you want to do?

You are now ready to begin creating plans to achieve *The Ideal* life. If you have read the previous pages of this book, you now have the knowledge. Let's transform your knowledge into wisdom by investing a few moments jotting down your top three **SELF-goals** on the next four pages.

Top 3 Goals for My Spiritual Self:

1. _____

_____

_____

2. _____

_____

_____

3. _____

_____

_____

Remember: Goals should be:

Specific

Measureable

Action-oriented

Realistic

Time-based

Top 3 Goals for My Emotional Self:

1. _____

_____

_____

2. _____

_____

_____

3. _____

_____

_____

Remember: Goals should be:

Specific

Measureable

Action-oriented

Realistic

Time-based

Top 3 Goals for My Logical Self:

1. _____

_____

_____

2. _____

_____

_____

3. _____

_____

_____

Remember: Goals should be:

Specific

Measureable

Action-oriented

Realistic

Time-based

Top 3 Goals for My Finite Self:

1. _____

_____

_____

2. _____

_____

_____

3. _____

_____

_____

Remember: Goals should be:

Specific

Measureable

Action-oriented

Realistic

Time-based

No matter how deep the valley...

No matter how tall the mountain...

Set goals. Make plans.

Achieve your dreams.

∼5∼

Find and Follow a Philosopher

This world is filled with a wealth of experience.

Some of those experiences occurred last week and last year. Some of those experiences occurred hundreds of years ago. Sir Isaac Newton published notes on many of his brilliant and world-changing experiences, as did Plato, Socrates, Niccolò Machiavelli, Epicurus, Jesus of Nazareth (via the Apostles), and one of my personal favorite, Marcus Aurelius.

Each of these great philosophers left a profound mark on the world by publicly stating and sharing their respective philosophies. Yet their published works will go unseen, unread, and unappreciated by most people. Despite having a prolific and terrific sense of seemingly supernatural wisdom, these philosophers and many of their teachings will go unnoticed by the vast majority of people.

Why?

Time and time again, I hear pessimistic people say, *"There is no instruction book for life."* Yet, these same people do not seek the instructions of some of the wisest sages who ever walked the earth. In reality, the aforementioned philosophers were more than just wise men; they were mighty mental mentors, immensely informed intellectuals, and tremendously talented teachers.

Their **philosophies** changed the world.

But what is it about the word ***philosophy*** and its implied academic doctrine that turns so many of us away from proven, prudent instruction that can positively affect our ever-evolving lives forever?

The answer is usually rooted in fear. As is the case with calculus, cooking, and constant change, many people fear what they don't understand. Instead of investing a little time to seek and understand *philosophy*, many people prefer to waste valuable time denouncing the one thing that can change their lives: *tested and tried philosophies.*

And to be sure, we must be very careful when choosing, tasting, and nurturing ourselves on another person's philosophy. This could be risky.

However, to ***change*** is to ***move from...***

And to ***move from*** your current rational spot to a whole new mental location, you must be exposed to new methods and manners of thinking, doing, and being. These methods might be as old as Methuselah. But they might also be new to you.

Make no mistake:
We all have our own philosophy.

Say it with me:

"I have my own philosophy."

But what *is* philosophy? And how can it help *you*?

The word *philosophy* comes from
the Greek φιλοσοφία (philosophia),
which literally means
love of wisdom. [1]

But what is *wisdom*?

Wisdom is the *application* (or *use*) of knowledge.

What is knowledge?

Knowledge is simply *retained information*; this includes facts, figures, and everything in this book.

To achieve **The Ideal**, we must learn to learn from others and ourselves. More importantly, we must do more than learn.   Yes, we must love the learning.   But most importantly, *we must love learning how to apply what we have learned*.

Your roadmap to achieve **The Ideal** life is now set.

Your purpose is to **move from** ...

...merely gaining and retaining information...
...to using and applying the knowledge...
...to loving the wisdom.

Re-stating the red words above in the fewer bold words below: Your purpose is to **move** ...

... from learning...
...to being wise...
...to using a new philosophy.

---

[1] *Philosophy: Adapted from Wikipedia.org. Retrieved September 3 2011 from http://en.wikipedia.org/wiki/Philosophy.*

In the final analysis, *loving wisdom* is simply *loving what is*. This is not to say that we have to love all the horrible things that happen at any time in our lengthy lives (or in the lives of our closest friends, nearest neighbors, or evil enemies).

Regardless of whether or not you like or agree with what "is..." sooner or later you will have to accept it. By crossing the threshold from **denial** to **acceptance**, you can then begin to adapt to almost any event. *To adapt* is "to change." To successfully adapt, we must first accept and understand that change is inevitable. And when something is inevitable, it is literally unstoppable.

It is also predictable... Change *will* occur.

If, then, you cannot work to stop change, you must learn how to make change work for you. Moreover, the likelihood of creating a successful change event increases exponentially when you focus on changing your SELF. Stop trying to change other people and their respective perspectives. Leave that effort to the philosophers who you have yet to learn from and apply their teachings. Instead, focus on finding a philosopher.

Don't blindly follow, swallow, or hollow out your own life-learned knowledge. However, once you find **your** philosopher, use his or her philosophy as a seed to grow your own philosophical garden.

By using other philosophies to grow your own viewpoint, you will quickly learn what may have taken years for other philosophers to yearn, learn, and discern. More importantly, by considering other philosophies, you not only help shape your priorities and presentations, you also become a lover of wisdom... You become a true philosopher.

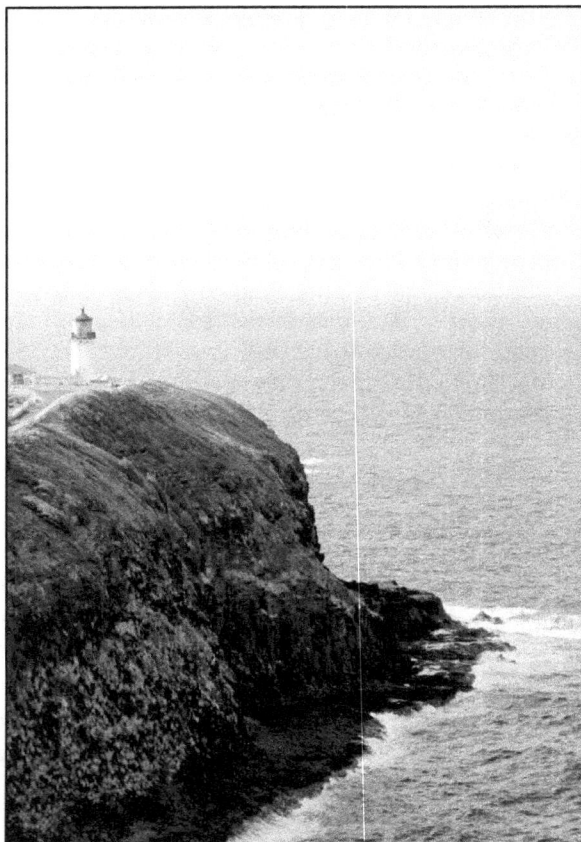

Find a philosopher.

Use those teachings.

Seed your own philosophy.

Launch your new life.

~**6**~

Forgive. Focus. Find.

Have you ever had someone accidentally step on you foot, and then keep on walking as if they had not harmed you? Most of us have had this or some other similar "accident" occur. Interestingly, all we ever really want is an acknowledgement, right?

What's the first thing we say when (after stepping on our foot) someone says, "*Oh, I'm sorry.*"(?) We usually say something like, "*Oh... that's ok!*"

Really? It's ok? Well, by that logic, someone can step on our foot over and over again. And as long as the offender(s) apologize, we'd be a-ok with our foot getting stomped on repeatedly. Yeah... *right!*

Of course, this is not true. But it *does* raise an interesting truism: When we are hurt, harmed, or hindered by others, we want an acknowledgment from the offenders. We want proof that they know how much they have hurt us. Right?

Well... if you **really** want to achieve *The Ideal* life, simply skip the middleman, and fore-give them the apology. You have already seen this advice earlier in this book. And there is a very good reason I am re-stating it here: Stop wasting time dwelling on what other people *should* do.

Instead, focus your attention and energy on finding the activities that make your heart sing. Forgive yourself for every stupid little thing you have ever done. And forgive all those stupid people, too. **Focus on you.** Apologies don't make you happy. You make you happy. Ready? Set? *Go!*

Forgive. Focus. Find.

Looking back, you can learn.

Standing still, you can focus.

Looking forward, you can dream.

Start by giving self-forgiveness first.

~7~

Define. Design. Align.

Preview The New You

Regardless of where you are...
Regardless of what you are doing...
Irrespective of your social circle...
In every situation *The Ideal* is possible.

In every situation, these 5 elements exist:

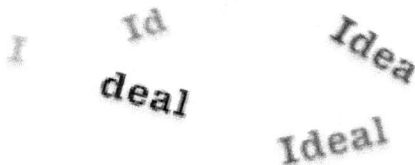

I   Id   Idea   deal   Ideal

Life is an experiment. You can actually do whatever you want to do! And, if for some crazy (or sane) reason you want to change your life, likes, or life-long job... do it! Life is an experiment!

You are the one who defines your life. **You** are the one who creates the blueprint for your life. Ultimately, you are the one who aligns your priorities, powers, and potentialities to persevere in a world where positivity can be in short supply.

You are the only one who is ***totally responsible*** to define, design, and align your life to the way that *you* want it to be. As presented in *The Clark Model of Life Leadership*, though some people will address your habits, and many others will attempt to set your priorities, it is ***your* view** (presentation) of the world that matters most.

What do YOU think?

What do YOU see?

Ask yourself these important questions:

Who am I ?

What does my Id say about my life?

What is my IDEA of an IDEAL life?

You define, design, and align all aspects of your life. The blueprint for your design is often drawn from friends, family, television shows, movies, magazines, and massive ad campaigns from multinational companies. Now, more than ever, there are numerous books available to delve into the specific issues of your neighbor, your nationality, or your spouse. However, *this* page of *this* book is all about you. On this page, I ask you two very simple questions:

1. How long will you tell the same old story?
2. When will you start a whole new life?

Only you can initiate the solution to your problems. Regardless of what happens, you are (still) able to respond in any way you choose. However, many people struggle to prevail over the greedy Id, the evil ego, or the simple hurt we feel in response to the treatment we receive from others. If we can somehow remember that we *always* have a vast array of choices on how we can potentially respond to a situation, we can overcome the Id, the ego, and the pride within.

I Id Idea
deal Ideal

When we conquer the Id, we have a clear picture in our mind's eye. When we overcome the Id, we see more clearly those *better* ideas on how to best handle the situation. Armed with a clear picture of possible ideas, we can then make the best deal with our thoughts and reality. The best possible deal between thoughts and reality is **The Ideal.**

de·fine *(verb)*

1. To state precisely the meaning of.
2. To describe the essential qualities of.
3. To determine the boundary or extent of.

When *you* define *your* self, you are stating exactly what you are. You are describing the essential qualities that make you who you *are* and *will be*.

When defining who you are, also consider who and what *you are not*. By considering who you are not, you not only reveal your limits and limitation of resources, you also better understand where some of your energy is often wasted. Basketball superstar Michael Jordan dabbled in other sports after his first retirement from the NBA. And though he signed a contract with the Chicago White Sox, he excelled in the sport of his greatest skill, effort, and energy: basketball.

As you begin your quest for *The Ideal*, invest a week pondering and developing honest answers to the following self-defining questions:

~ What are my greatest strengths?
~ What are my physical and mental assets?
~ What are my self-admitted liabilities?
~ What do I (currently) really *need* in life?
~ What do I (currently) really *want* in life?
~ What do I absolutely *not want* in my life?
~ Where will I be in 5 years? How will I get there?
~ What would my eulogy say if given tomorrow?
~ What do I want my eulogy to say when I die?

Did you notice what's missing from the questions? The word *who* is not there. Other people don't define you. Only you define you.

> **de·sign** *(verb)*
>
> **1.** To plan and make artistically or skillfully.
> **2.** To form or conceive in the mind; to invent.
> **3.** To intend, as for a specific purpose; to plan.

After considering *who and what you are not,* turn your total focus toward *being* the best that you are… and *becoming* the best that you *can be.* Don't waste time, energy, or effort avoiding this, that, and the other. Racecar drivers don't *avoid starting lines;* they focus solely on The Finish Line.

We are all headed to an eventual finish line.

And though you are probably not a racecar driver, you are definitely on a journey that has already begun, and you are undeniably speeding toward the finish line. Accordingly, design your life with the end in mind. Focus your life-design efforts on the four parts of self that, when properly nurtured and fed, will surely lead you to the victory lane.

Invest a few days pondering and developing the answers to these five SELF-designing questions:

1. How can I explain **Spiritual** parts of me?
2. How do I describe **Emotional** well-being?
3. How can I adopt a **Logical**, balanced life?
4. What **are** my own **Finite** limitations?
5. How can I best prepare for my day, week, & life?

Use answers to the first four questions above to answer the most important fifth question. By defining success on your terms, you can then design a life, one day at a time – each day created specifically for your own SELF-success.

a·lign *(verb)*

1. To arrange in a line or so as to be parallel.
2. To adjust to produce a proper relationship.
3. To ally yourself with one side of an argument.

1. To arrange in a line or so as to be parallel.

After a few weeks of sincere SELF-evaluation, the path toward re-defining and re-designing your self will become abundantly clear. In fact, once you answer the questions on the two previous pages, you will have already created your very own unique blueprint to build **The Ideal** life. This blueprint includes a drumbeat of decisions to dictate your distant destination by directing a delicate dance amidst your daily dreams, dares, cares, and scares. This blueprint is a beginning. However, you must do more than define & design.

2. To adjust to produce a proper relationship;

To achieve **The Ideal** life, simply follow the rhyme: **Define – Design – Align.** These three steps help build a healthy SELF-relationship. In fact, achieving **The Ideal** life is impossible unless you understand the concepts of interrelation, integration, and sublimation of energy and matter.

Huh? What is sublimation of energy and matter?

Without going into a huge science lesson on the essence of Einstein's often misunderstood *Theory of Relativity* and the more well-known equation $e=MC^2$, you are simply required to know this:

It matters what you put your energy into.

3. To ally your SELF with one side of an argument.

To make any degree of success toward achieving *The Ideal* life, you will have to take a long, hard look at **E V E R Y T H I N G** you do and ask yourself one significant, super-simple question:

> Does this action
> (and every action I do)
> # PROMOTE
> or
> # PREVENT
> *momentum* toward my
> self-defined, self-designed
> ideal life?

In theory, everything you do should promote your plan. Everything you do should encourage you. Indeed, your actions should add courage to your sense of self and *The Ideal* life. Beginning with your initial two broad-based actions to define and design a new life, each one of *your* successive actions uses *your* energy, and, more importantly, has the potential to further increase *your* power.

You must focus your powers on your plan.

Now's the time... Define. Design. Align!

~❽~

Review. Rewind. Re-Mind.

Re·view. No matter what people say to you... **it's just data.** It's facts, figures, fibs, flagrant fabrications, and fantastic fantasies that are rarely ever true. Interestingly, when people say bad things about other people, nothing really changes. So why say bad things about other people? In fact, why say bad things about *anything*? Wouldn't it be better to accept people for who they are... while making yourself better than you were? Better yet: Wouldn't it be best to see the world from an idealistic point of view? This is **The Ideal**.

Re·wind. There are many ways to relax. Some people rewind on the couch while watching television; other people rewind with physical exercise. For the purposes of achieving **The Ideal,** rewind means *re-energize*. And like the little wind-up toys of our youth, we, too, require an occasional re-winding of our internal workings.

Re·mind. The purpose of this book is to help you see a different point of view. However, this book is just a guide. On the path of life, you are the driver. You control the direction, the speed, and the ultimate destination. As you create your path, remember: When you increase the **number** and the **percentage** of happy thoughts in your mind, you are much more likely to select a happy thought when you are faced with an unhappy situation in life. Re-mind yourself today!

Review

Refine

Remind

~9~

Accept. Adapt. Achieve.

In 1968, 9-1-1 became the national emergency telephone number in the United States. In was theorized that calling one well-known number was the best path to providing ***immediate*** access to police, fire and ambulance services. [1]

When you think about it, the 9-1-1 concept is a simple-but-powerful tool for not only emergency management officials, but also for you, me, and anyone else who wants the security of immediate access to police, fire and ambulance services.

Likewise, the concept of **accepting, adapting,** and **achieving** our everyday goals is also simple.

But can it be considered "powerful?"
Yes: It is *very* powerful.

We can always **talk** about what we will do if this, that, or the other happens (when we are properly prepared and have the right tools). We can forever chant platitudes while sitting in a cozy prayer room, standing in a magic meditation closet, or kneeling at the alter of a safe and secure church.

However, our toughest battles don't occur in the convenient confines of cozy rooms, comfy closets, or cherished churches. Our toughest battles usually occur when we least expect it:

NOW!

---

[1] *9-1-1. In Wikipedia. Retrieved September 23, 2011, from http://en.wikipedia.org/wiki/9-1-1*

To face our toughest battles, we need a mantra:

Accept. Adapt. Achieve. ®

Similar to having one well-known telephone number for immediate access to police, fire and ambulance services, we need one well-known mantra for immediate access to a reminder that we are able to respond ideally to almost anything.

But first, we must accept what *is*.

Each and every minute of every day, as we seek the best path along our unknown journey in life, we must increase our appreciation for the twists and turns we will encounter along the way.

And just like our physical journey... we can't simply give up when we encounter washed-out roads or burned-out bridges. We can't simply give up when we face changes to our planned path, and the road ahead appears hopelessly blocked.

But sometimes we mortals need a little boost of power to help us believe and eventually see the path awaiting our presence on the other side of the troubled horizon. Sometimes we need a subtle reminder to help us acquire the faith to know *a bend in the road is not the end of the road unless we fail to make the all-important turn!*

Remember: *The Ideal* life is not in our past. Our past is gone forever. *The Ideal* life is right in front of us. And the *here and now* is not only *here and now,* it's also our greatest gift. We *now* have the time to make the most important decisions in our life. But what are the most important decisions?

Which decisions are more important than others?

Actually, every decision you make has the potential to create a life-changing event. The decision to take *this* taxicab or *that* taxicab ultimately affects every subsequent moment in your life. Your seemingly simple decision to get out of bed at 6:01 A.M. instead of 6:02 A.M. ultimately affects every other minute in your remaining life. Indeed, everything you do affects others and yourself in ways you will never be able to fully comprehend, predict, or prepare for.

What, then, *can* we do?

Remember: *The Ideal* life is not based on changing your external circumstances or other people. *The Ideal* life is based on three little words. The first of these words is such a simple concept: Accept.

---

ac·cept *(verb)*

1. To take or receive (something offered).
2. To agree or consent to; accede to.

Acceptance is something we are all capable of doing every day. In fact, you have already accepted the idea that this book could potentially change your life (hence your decision to open the cover and start reading the words herein).

However, many of us feel challenged when we have to accept things, events, situations, or people beyond our control. Interestingly, as stated in the definition of *accept*, acceptance is based on *your* approval or consent.

Nevertheless, the day's weather is not based on your consent; yet you wholeheartedly accept it.

Likewise, the number of Tuesdays, Sundays, Fridays, and Saturdays in each week are not based on your approval, agreement, or consent. Yet, you have accepted the concept of a day, week, month, and year. More importantly, you have **adapted** your life to and around these simple concepts.

What's my point?

In the final analysis, we make deals with our thoughts. We all make deals with our "SELFs." We simply *choose* to accept whatever we *think* we want to accept. Moreover, regardless of what we say, think, and do, this big lumbering globe we call earth will still keep on turning.

No matter what you say, think, or do... life goes on.

The best we can do is accept what has happened, adapt to it with the best of our abilities, and then move on.

In every journey throughout the world, we all live by the same basic law:

Accept. Adapt. Achieve. ®

Interestingly, *acceptance* is mostly about what has happened. *Adapting* is mostly about what *is* happening. And *achieving* is mostly about what *will* happen. But to truly understand the power of this great law, (accept, adapt, achieve), consider the opposite of each individual word:

Accept/Deny ~ **Adapt**/Maintain ~ **Achieve**/Fail

When we refuse to accept certain Truths, we plant the roots of our life in the world of denial.

de·ni·al *(noun)*

1. The rejection of the truth of a proposition.
2. *A psychological process by which painful truths are not admitted into your consciousness.*

In the definitions above, denial is based on a simple decision or a seemingly harmless choice. For example, smokers are the only ones who can choose to remain in denial about the horrific effects of smoking. It's their life; it's their choice.

Likewise, you are the only one who can decide how much of the present you want to spend dissecting and trying to rearrange the past.

But acceptance is not just about the past. What about today's truths? On what daily or weekly activities do you waste valuable time while pretending those activities are worth your time?

You are the only one who can *choose to* admit painful truths into your consciousness.

You are the one who can do almost anything if you:

1.   *Accept* a few facts.
2.   *Adapt* your life to those facts.
3.   Achieve what you want.

Though I have previously stressed the importance of the fist step of **acceptance**, the first question to ask your *SELF* is related to the third maxim:

"What do I really want to achieve?"

∾ 10 ∾

Be A Positive Information Exchange

Oscar Wilde, an Irish playwright, poet and author, is often quoted as saying, "Some cause happiness **wherever** they go; others **whenever** they go."

What are some of **your** best-known quotes?
Better yet, which of "those people" are you?
Do you cause happiness when **coming** or **going**?

If you don't know the answer to this question, you are either in denial... or the answer is along the lines of "You cause happiness **whenever** you go."

Beginning today, you can change everything.

How?

Simply become a positive information exchange!

How?

Make it your specific mission to share only the best possible news with your friends, family, and anyone else who has the pleasure of sharing the same intersection of space and time with you.

Why do this?

The world is filled with negative people, nasty news, and not-so-good stories about life. Every time you see another person, you have an opportunity to literally change their world. So if you really want to find happiness, create it at every single opportunity... no matter where you are or whom you're with. **There**, you will find it.

When presented with the simple advice to *"give happiness,"* many people say they are afraid of what other people might say, think, or do. Such concerns are made up of a made-up thing called fear. And the best way to deal with fear is with another made-up entity called faith.

Everything in life requires faith. This small statement of truth is profound on a level that most people simply do not understand. Every single act that you do on a daily basis… is an act of faith.

We have faith the sun will rise next Tuesday. We have faith in the corner store being open… especially when we "need" that store to be open.

We have faith that our cousins, brothers, sisters, and all of our other relatives will grow old with us. We have faith that the government will be intact when the worst possible things occur. We have faith that our personal interpretation of the facts is an accurate representation of reality.

And in one way or another, we have faith that the worst case scenario (whatever it is) will either 1) not occur; or 2) not occur to us; or 3) if it does occur to us, we can somehow, someway get past it.

Indeed, everything in life requires faith.

No matter what has happened; no matter what *will* happen, our situation is not an end, but rather a whole new beginning. And with a little (more) faith and a (lot more) focus on the positive aspects of life, we can achieve the best, most awesome, wonderful thing in the world. We can achieve something called *The Ideal*. But first, we must choose to accept one simple methodology for life: we must choose to Accept. Adapt. Achieve. ®

Part 7: The Directions

Clean Your Glasses

When preparing for a long road trip, it's a good idea to clean the windows of the vehicle. As the trip continues, the windows become somewhat soiled. And to keep the vehicle and its occupants safe, it's wise to periodically clean the windshield. The vehicle's rear window might also be dirty, but it's not the rear view that matters most. The front view provides the most important viewpoint.

Likewise, our bodies are the vehicles for our souls.

And the same safe-travels concepts apply to our journey in life: As it's often said, *"Our eyes are the windows to the soul."* Thus, let's cherish the road on which we have travelled. However, let's not waste our time focusing on what **has** happened.

Let's focus on the road ahead.

As we know: Days will come and go. The sun will set, and night will slowly but surely seep in. We are often left wondering where the day went. And for many of us, merely *reflecting* on the previous day can be as challenging as the day itself. As we focus forward, we must learn to periodically clean our glasses. In real-world terms, we must not wait until the end of the day to re-energize. With all the technology, traffic, and tests we face throughout the day, a proactive and practical approach to **The Ideal** life is the best strategy to use. This chapter is essentially a step-by-step guide created to proactively clean your rose-colored glasses throughout the day and week.

Start, maintain, and end your day with these 10 practical steps...

Clean Your Glasses

Meditate
Dedicate
Separate
Educate
Integrate
Pollinate
Incinerate
Rejuvenate
Illuminate
Congratulate

Your life is actually one specific event. However...

The earth rotates on its axis, creating the concepts we have been taught to refer to as day and night. Similarly, the earth orbits the sun, creating the concept we have been taught to refer to as seasons. We, *mankind*, have taken our long, lovely lives and divided those lives into segments according to rotations of the earth itself... and annual revolutions of the earth around the sun.

Of course, you already know this.

But do you realize the awesome power of using these known concepts to literally change your life?

Do you understand the fact that *day* and *night* don't really exist? Do you now understand that day and night are just concepts that we have been taught to see, believe, and *know* how to use in the one, big, long life that we have been given?

Obviously, we will never convince the rest of the world that *day* and *night* are mere concepts.

However, we can use those same concepts as a _foundational framework of focused transformation._

We can use the mere concepts of day and night to help us realize that life, as one specific event, can actually be viewed as thousands of connected components. Each of these linked components, (connected only by you - and no one else), is actually **interdependently** created by you and others. This concept of interdependence must be fully understood before reading the next step.

From Wikipedia:
Interdependence is the dynamic of being mutually and physically responsible to, and sharing a common set of principles with others.

This concept differs distinctly from "dependence," which implies that each member of a relationship cannot function or survive apart from one another.

In an interdependent relationship, all participants are emotionally, economically, ecologically and/or morally self-reliant while at the same time responsible to each other. An interdependent relationship can be defined as one that depends on two or more cooperative autonomous participants.

Interdependence recognizes the truth in each position and weaves them together. [1]

Why is this concept of _interdependence_ so important to this particular ideal _(Clean Your Glasses)?_ What does _interdependence_ have to do with day and night? And how can this concept get you to **The Ideal** life?

---

[1]Interdependence. (n.d.). In Wikipedia. Retrieved August 21, 2011, from http://en.wikipedia.org/wiki/Interdependence

The answer to each of those questions is based on the fact that your past has the potential to have almost nothing to do with your future.

The above fact is actually a double-edge sword.

In other words, disconnecting your past from your future can be a good thing or a bad thing for you.

You could have been a millionaire last year, and financially bankrupt tomorrow. Likewise, you could have been the picture of perfect health last night, and end up on life support in the hospital emergency room sometime next week.

On the other hand, you could have been financially bankrupt last year, and be well on your way to a vast financial fortune by the end of next year. Indeed, you could be broke, busted, and disgusted today… and footloose and fancy-free next week.

You could be in the midst of horrifically bad physical health today… and soon star in your own unbelievably real and miraculous comeback story before the end of next month. It's true: Literally and figuratively, you could be flat on your back today, and, yet, standing tall just a few short weeks from now. Stranger things have happened.

So what's my point?

Though connected by the long life that is you, each of your individually lived days is totally different, dissimilar, divergent, diverse, and distinctive. You will never have the same day as today. In fact, every single one of your days is so dramatically different and distinctive from the others… it is literally impossible to have the same day twice.

Accordingly, each day is a vast ocean of opportunity, unlike anything you have ever seen. Regardless of what opportunities you *think* you may have missed yesterday, last month, or several years ago, today is so much better than yesterday.

Today is the day you accept, adapt, and creatively achieve the framework that goes far beyond the concept of day and night. Today is the day you take a step back, look at your life, and realize a powerful point of truth: Though there are no days, nights, hours, or minutes, you are taught to live according to the calendar, clock, and watch.

And though the calendar, clock, and watch may appear to measure something called *time*, the only time that has ever existed is *now*. The only time that will *ever* exist is *now*. Accordingly, beginning today, you will leverage the calendar, watch, and clock to measure how well you treasure the most valuable asset you will ever have: NOW. How?

Well, thus far, you have used this book as a guide along your path to **The Ideal** life. In Part 1, you read about *Transitions and Traditions*. In Part 2, you discovered *Four Little Questions*. Part 3 asked you to consider a series of *Three Little Words*. Part 4 was all about *Your Next Steps*. In Part 5, you learned about *How to Get There*. And Part 6 covered *Your Ideal Roadmap* and 10 specific steps.

Now it's time to shift gears. Here is where the rubber meets the road. This final part of **The Ideal** is focused squarely on the daily directions of *how*. And just like a grand land journey: If you really want to find and use the best route, use the knowledge found in a good map. The previous pages of **The Ideal** have focused on providing knowledge for your current journey. However...

As stated in **Knowledge versus Wisdom**, let's not confuse knowledge with a lack of wonderful wisdom. You could have the best roadmap in the world. But if you decide not to use your roadmap, so much of what you have will be wasted. Remember the differences...

---

knowl·edge *(noun)*

- The state or fact of knowing

---

wis·dom *(noun)*

- Utilizing knowledge, understanding and insight

Here's the Idea:
*Wisdom is the **application** of knowledge.*

Here's the Deal:
*Knowledge is not power until it is applied. When we **use** knowledge, we instantly become wise. Learn from this book. More importantly: do what it says!*

For the next 21 days, focus on the following 10 Ideals. These are specific roadmap directions. If you can successfully master just one of these daily directions, you can then master two... and then three. (I think you see where this is going).

Beginning today, you will have the knowledge to...

1.	Meditate	6.	Pollinate
2.	Dedicate	7.	Incinerate
3.	Separate	8.	Rejuvenate
4.	Educate	9.	Illuminate
5.	Integrate	10.	Congratulate

Use this knowledge to clean your glasses daily:

1. **Meditate:** Meditation is a powerful ritual you can use to launch a very successful day. Using a timer or a watch, begin this deliberate process to clear your mind.

    The first 15 minutes of every day could be *spent* worrying about this, that, and the other. Or you could *invest* 15 minutes clearing your mind, and preparing to receive and fill-up on positive, optimistic, and confident thoughts.

    Meditation is not prayer (though you could actually speak to yourself, your spiritual deity, or whatever best invigorates your spirit). Meditation is a focused effort to clear your mind and facilitate a conscious awareness of the various aspects of your SELF. You are not your thoughts. Meditation releases your thoughts and illuminates your spirit.

    Morning meditation is a particularly powerful and especially effective ritual because, it starts your day with you deciding which thoughts, decisions, actions, and tasks are most important.

    By agreeing to start your day with a total focus on you, and a deliberate process to clear your mind, you are prioritizing the importance of your time, your energy, and your body. You are telling the world, the calendar, the clock, and the watch, *"This is my day; I will start it how I choose. And though every single minute of the remaining day might be interdependent upon others, my thoughts and my SELF matter more than anything else."*

2. **Dedicate:** Using a calendar, at least once a week, plan to commit yourself to something bigger than you. Focus your actions and thoughts on a person, an organization, or a cause that is beyond your individual capability to fully solve.

When you dedicate a part of your *SELF*, you do more than merely give a portion of the life force that is you... you actually *surrender* your energy to something outside of your *SELF*.

Indeed, *surrender* is a very powerful concept. Because of a mostly negative connotation, the very **thought** and subsequent **act** of surrendering can be a very scary process for many people.

However, *surrender* is more about voluntary relinquishment of control than it is about loss or forfeiture of power. And when you cheerfully and consistently voluntarily give yourself (and your energy) to an effort, cause, organization, or event that exists largely outside of your concern for your *SELF*, you will reap considerable returns on your investment.

And though these returns are not likely to be tangible or readily available for your immediate use, when you dedicate yourself to something bigger than you, interestingly enough, you become part of that same larger-than-life effort, cause, organization, or event. Thus your *SELF* becomes larger than life. *You* become larger than life. You create a legacy that will last long after you are no longer here.

3. **Separate:** Using the hourly chimes from a clock or a watch, take a long, deep breath and ask yourself *how* you are thinking. Literally think or verbally ask yourself, *"Am I thinking positively?"*

If your thoughts were already positive, simply renew, refresh, and rejuvenate your previously positive thoughts. On the other hand, if your thoughts were previously negative, simply separate the past from the present and ask yourself, *"Why am I being negative?"*

This is an important question. As stated in the chapter *Knowledge versus Wisdom*, *"When you understand thought and emotion, you create a pathway between knowledge and wisdom; you literally create a solution with the one thing in this world that you control: YOU."*

By increasing awareness of your SELF, you are better informed on what makes you tick, what makes you sick, and which habits you should kick. This is good info!

Remember: Negative thoughts can't exist in the same thought-space as positive thoughts. Unfortunately, throughout the day, external media can influence (and sometimes create) many of our negative thoughts. Television shows, talk radio, pop culture, and people have a very formative impact on how you think. Learn to identify your influential input *(Ones and Zeros)* and invest time and effort in separating yourself from the negative influences (especially people).

4. **Educate**: Using a calendar and a clock, invest 15 minutes a day to capture specific and random thoughts in a journal. Keeping a journal can help you achieve a whole new level of self-awareness.

First, by penning random and specific thoughts, you will soon have a historical record of the various actions, events, people, and thoughts that seem to affect you the most. Secondly, when you write your thoughts, you will most likely better understand and focus on what you are *really* thinking and feeling.

Many consumers don't like to take surveys. However, if a customer feels very strongly about a particular product or service, they are far more likely to complete a survey. Interestingly enough, *likelihood of response* is not dependent on whether or not the customer's experience was negative or positive. The most important factor is **how strongly** the customer feels about the experience. Similarly, over time, a journal will begin to shed an honest light on the people and things that seem to affect you the most.

Lastly, you can use your journal to jot down a few notes of thankfulness. When you appreciate something, it appreciates in value. And when writing about the things for which you are thankful, you are creating a personal pick-me-up that can be used to nurture and inspire yourself on some future day when you need it most. In a very real way, you are creating the solution to your own distant challenge.

5. **Integrate:** Using a calendar as a planner, proactively select, place, and use a positive word or phrase for every day of the week. Find a way to incorporate that word/phrase/action into the entire day by making it your foundation for optimistic thought and positive growth from breakfast until well after dinner.

More than a simple act of *combining words, integration* is all about threading various items in and around one focused point. I call this concept **blueprinting**, and it's essentially the same concept as choosing the foundation for a building, and then getting started on the process of building the building. As discussed earlier in *The Elevator of Life:*

"If we can start with one beautiful choice, we can set forth a wonderfully positive day. That wonderfully positive day can actually be partnered with a subsequently successful day, until... before we know it, the week has been a smashing success, and the month is an overwhelming triumph."

When you start with a positive foundation and build upon that foundation with positive thoughts and actions, you are literally creating a perpetual path of positive thought. You are setting the stage for an awesome production starring you and a successful trend upwards. And by using a calendar to plan and place your positive power, you are harnessing the concept of time, and leveraging days, weeks, and months to work *for* you and your goal to achieve *The Ideal* life.

6. **Pollinate:** Using your watch as a trigger, "re-mind" yourself to ask yourself a very timely question: *When was the last time I was proactively positive to someone?*

(If you don't currently own a watch, perhaps it' a *good time* to buy one...)

Instead of allowing your watch to pummel, push, and prod you to the next event, meeting, action, or potential pounding, THINK of your watch as a little friend who has many different jobs.

Yes, he (or she) is there to help you split the day into 24 neat little chunks of time.

Yes, your little wrist pal is there to make sure you and everyone else in the world is within the same zone of time (now).

Pollinate... From this day forward, your watch can help you remember to plant a thoughtful seed of positivity in everyone, everywhere you go. Your watch can be a **reminder** that we find happiness wherever we give it. Accordingly, when you look at your watch, simply smile at the next person you see. Whenever you see someone else's watch, tell them it's a nice watch... and give them a free smile.

Moreover, your watch can now be used to prompt you to simply take a deep breath, exhale, smile, and know that this, too, shall pass. Equally important: After you send a smile or any other kind gesture to someone, you have just proactively pollinated a seed of perpetual positivity.

7. **Rejuvenate:** Using your existing dining times, invest three short minutes reinvigorating and redirecting your thoughts and emotions toward a positive mindset. Use breakfast, lunch, and dinner to revive more than just your body; use these times to restart the clock on measuring how successful you have been at maintaining a positive outlook on life.

The name of this book implies the lofty goal of achieving an "almost perfect" life. However, perfection does not exist. And the quest for *The Ideal* life is a continuous quest; it is not something we complete and subsequently cease all effort toward... it is a life-long dream.

In fact, *The Ideal* life is an existence; a life; an alignment of your energies toward an acceptance and eventual understanding that the path of life is not smooth. It is meandering, unstable, and sometimes jagged, ragged, if not outright tattered and torn with discontent, disdain, and downright damning downpours of one disappointment after another.

Yet, the time we share does not stop.
The clock of our lives keeps ticking.
What, then, are we to do?

Rejuvenate. And we must do this often. Mealtime, while feeding the body, is the perfect time to rejuvenate the mind and soul. Why not invest a mere 180 seconds and feed all three at the same time? Spend your mealtime thinking about how blessed you are to have what you have.

8. **Illuminate**: Using a calendar as a guide, practice proactive planning for positive presentations. In other words, at least once a month, proactively seek new input to your positively skewed, renewed mind.

    This new input could be a new book of positive poetry, an old book on optimistic thoughts, or even the very old Book of Proverbs, or other proverbial books (as written by various historical, proverbial or philosophical leaders).

    Your new input could be a short lunch with a friend who always seems to have a sunny disposition. Your new input could be an extended meditation session that you choose to set aside specifically to receive new input from your deepest sense of self.

    As discussed in the earlier chapter, *Priorities. Propensities. Presentations… "To truly change your priorities, you must see the need to change your priorities. In order to see the need to change your priorities, you must have the proper perspective. To change your habits, you must see the need to change your habits. To see the need to change your habits, you must have the proper perspective."*

    As you begin to incorporate new input into your positively skewed mind, your path will soon change toward an even brighter landscape, offering greater opportunities to get, give, and grow. Surely, you can set aside one day a month for such a grand opportunity as this!

9. **Incinerate**: At bedtime, remind yourself that the day is over. The day's events are now a part of history.

    Accept the fact that changes have occurred. Accept the fact that the effect of those changes will someday be affected by additional changes that have not yet become a part of our reality.

    Adapt to the fact that you, your mind, body, and spirit are the result of millions and millions of tiny little changes that have occurred throughout your lifetime.

    Achieve conclusion of effort toward resolution of the day's problems by simply jotting thoughts down in your journal and forgetting about them for a smidgen of time... long enough for your mind, body, and soul to rest together, if but for one night. Of course, there will be those events that will forever alter the course of your life. Physical and emotional injuries, and untimely deaths of people we love are especially tragic. Yet, the clock of our lives keeps ticking. Thus, we are left with a choice to accept and adapt... or live in denial and maintain the heavy sense of loss associated with those specific tragedies. And for the most hurtful events, we must *choose* to allow the setting sun to burn those experiences into our history, but not so much that we scorch our most prosperous present. Bedtime is a good time to give others and yourself an apology for the day's incidents that fell short of *The Ideal*. We must forego the guilt by fore-giving the apology.

10. **Congratulate**: Place meeting makers on your paper and electronic calendars. The subject of the meeting maker should be:

Congratulations!

In today's electronic world of spam mail, millions of emails have the subject line that simply says, "Congratulations!" And despite all the warnings about computer viruses and spam mail, we still fight the urge to open that email and see if we have actually won something of value.

Learn to leverage the part of our nature that longs to celebrate and appreciate. As you gain momentum toward achieving **The Ideal** life, schedule the opposite of what some people call a pity party; plan a Power Party. Coordinate a Commend Celebration. Organize an Optimistic Open House. Call it whatever you want... but *congratulate* yourself on moving from merely *learning* to becoming a lover of wisdom. Reinforce, reemphasize, and highlight your new philosophy.

Do not underestimate the power of self-exaltation. Indeed, others might look upon your newfound joy with doubt, disagreement, or even disdain. Some may say you "think you're all that."

Simply tell them:

Believing is one thing...

Knowing *is everything.*

Beginning today, I will…

Meditate

Dedicate

Separate

Educate

Integrate

Pollinate

Rejuvenate

Illuminate

Incinerate

Congratulate

I now have the knowledge.

* Download & print a FREE RE-MINDER at www.TheIdeal.com

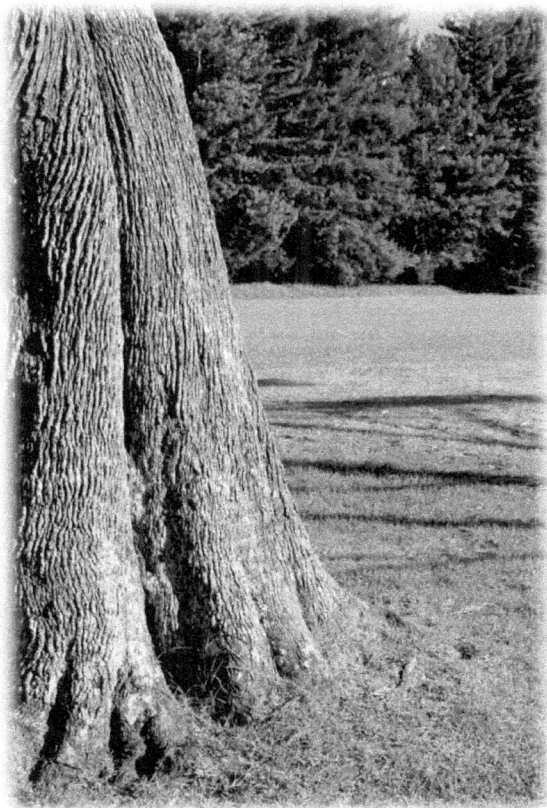

What is the foundation of your faith?

How deeply are you rooted in belief?

What are you accepting?

To what are you adapting?

The Final Analysis

The question is

What do you want to achieve?

The pages of this book encourage you to incorporate the mantra *Accept. Adapt. Achieve.* ®

When dealing with terrific or terrible situations, we seem to have the greatest difficulty with the first of these great life actions: **Accept.**

Without true acceptance of "what is," we are really dealing with a made-up, fictitious world. And without first accepting the truth that we, ourselves, have the greatest influence over our circumstances, we live at the risk of creating solutions that are not likely to succeed. And because these self-inflicted solutions are often based on denial, I must re-emphasize that we must never underestimate the power of denial. Instead, let's accept the reality of the situation. Then... we can immediately begin the second step in the mantra: **Adapt.**

Adapting is the very lifeblood of change. When we reach the *adapt* phase of the mantra, we are successfully dealing with reality... and *dealing in* a new reality. Yes, challenges will continue. But we are already on the road to success! Interestingly, the last part of the mantra, **Achieve**, is actually where we begin our journey to *successive* successes. In the final analysis, with the right roadmap, you have only one question to answer:

What do YOU want to achieve?

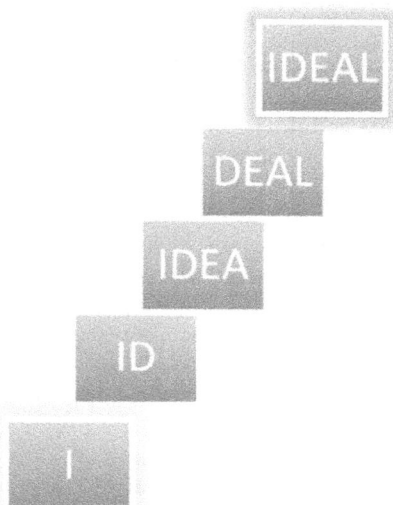

It all starts with **YOU**. You can achieve *The Ideal* life... one step at a time. After gaining true awareness of who YOU are, you will begin to gain better influence over the "id." Remember: According to Freud's psychoanalytic theory of personality, the **id** is the personality component made up of unconscious psychic energy that tries to gratify basic urges, needs, and desires. The **id** actually works on the "pleasure principle," demanding immediate gratification of needs.

However, instead of satisfying immediate urges, focus on populating your mind with the best ideas.

From your mind's universe of thoughts, you can draw upon ideas and make deals with the best part of your self. The best deals come from the best ideas. And the best ideas are created when you balance the **S**piritual, **E**motional, **L**ogical, and **F**inite aspects of you and your unique nature.

The Ideal

Your Guide to An Ideal Life

If you are genuinely interested in achieving **The Ideal** life, the roadmap and directions herein are relatively simple to implement in the seemingly complicated journey of life. Here's a review:

1. Obtain an accurate awareness of who you are.

2. Accept a few Truths about life.

3. Adapt to those Truths. Change is constant.

4. Achieve your dreams by setting daily, hourly, and monthly goals and plans to be positive.

5. Find and follow a philosopher.

6. Forgive. Focus. Find.
    a. Forgive yourself and others.
    b. Focus on today.
    c. Find your passion.

7. Preview The New You: Define. Design. Align.
    a. Define who you are.
    b. Design your life.
    c. Align your resources.

8. Review. Refine. Remind.

9. Accept. Adapt. Achieve. ®

10. Inspire. Be a positive information exchange.

11. Clean Your Glasses

By reading this book, you have begun a series of thought-provoking conversations within your deepest self. By obtaining an acute awareness of who you are, you can now see how you affect the world in which you and I live. Moreover, you can readily see how easy it is to positively affect the lives of every single person you meet.

As I have often said, *"The person in the mirror is the most important person in the world!"*

However, unfiltered looks in the mirror can be daunting, if not downright scary (not in terms of physical appearances, but in terms of seeing the type of person you are). Nonetheless, when it comes to seeing ourselves and other people for who we are, we must accept reality for what it is. Denial of the Truth, though easy and comfortable, really is an evil enemy of **The Ideal**.

On the other hand, if we stay true to the Truth and ourselves, we can learn how to readily adapt to reality. We must remember that change is the one constant that we can always count on. Accordingly, we, too, must constantly change.

We must not only *accept* our apparent imperfections, but we must also **embrace** them (along with our limitations, faults, weaknesses, and the fruits of our evil labor – some call this *Karma*). In terms of dealing with what "was," the best we can do is to forgive, focus, and find.

I rarely use the words "never" and "always." However, I assure you: We can never change what has already happened. But we can always forgive those people who have hurt, harmed, or hindered us... especially if that person is the one who knows more about us than anyone else: our SELF.

As soon as you learn the true meaning and application of fore-giveness, you literally create a whole new life by cutting the link that (only) you have been using as a pathway to the hurtful past.

As soon you learn the true meaning and application of fore-giveness, you literally create a whole new life; you sever the link to a hurtful past.

(Yes... that statement was worth repeating.)

Whether you are angry with an ex-spouse, ex-boss, or ex-kindergarten teacher, you alone have the power to set yourself free from the tyranny of additional anger, further fury, and repeated rage.

Forgive yourself and others, and then you can focus on today – the only day that actually exists.

When you see the astounding beauty and vast richness of life that is given to you with each successive day, you will soon find yourself drawn to certain courses of nature. You will begin to notice a path where there was previously only pain. You will hear music in what were mostly mundane melodies of morbid melancholy.

In short, you will find your passion.

Only you will know what that passion is.

Only you will know how it defines who you are.

And only you will know how to design your life around your newfound passion. The world and its inhabitants may never understand why you do what you do. So be prepared to face direct challenges to what you **know** is your destiny.

Be prepared to align your resources to facilitate your newfound passion. And regardless of the naysayers, negativity, and not-so-good responses, press onward, toward, and forward to what **you** want to achieve. In due time, you will review your goals, refine your plans, and remind yourself of what life was like before you changed it to *The Ideal* life.

The best way to review, refine, and remind yourself is through a daily period of rest and refresh. If you can do this on a daily basis... you will be very impressed with your results.

Ultimately, as you start this new journey, you will no longer use the word "*remind*" in the same way.

From this point forward, you will use the word *remind* to mean the literal changing of your mind. And as you go forward in your daily activities, you will constantly re-mind yourself into an inspirational positive information exchange.

You can now say to yourself:

I can control my Id.

I am making a deal with my best ideas.

In my deal with my best ideas...

I create *The Ideal*.

Congratulations...
Welcome to *The Ideal* Life!

You now have the knowledge.

Open the door and step forward.

Use this knowledge to create *The Ideal*!

Famous Last Words

We have all heard the saying, *"When one door closes, another one opens."* In reality, by the time that door has closed, the other door was already open for quite some time. We just didn't see it...

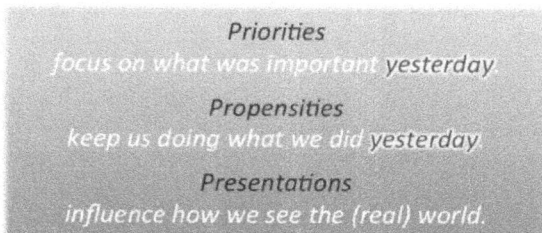

> *Priorities*
> *focus on what was important yesterday.*
>
> *Propensities*
> *keep us doing what we did yesterday.*
>
> *Presentations*
> *influence how we see the (real) world.*

Take a breather today and look all around you.

There is a vast network of unseen connections.

There are physical networks, yes.

But there are also emotional, spiritual, professional, familial, local, international, natural and, yes... supernatural attachments that link you with me, us with them, and everybody, everywhere on some level of interconnectedness. Our links can cause seemingly remote actions in one part of our world to affect the lives of people in an area geographically distant but supernaturally close. We are never *that* far apart.

Make it your priority to make it a habit to change world perceptions... by first changing you.

Whether you are seeking additional money, better relationships, improved health, or any other tangible asset, the same principles and universal laws apply to everyone, everywhere.

Interestingly, in recent years, there has been an increase in discussions regarding the *Law of Attraction*, manifesting destiny, and quantum physics. Each of these theories postulates similar concepts. Specifically, these theories suggest your life experience will ultimately match your beliefs. However, I strongly disagree with such simple, linear statements. Remember: "Believing is one thing; knowing is everything."

Accordingly, the *Law of Attraction*, manifesting destiny, and quantum physics all stop short of the magic cure. You must do more than merely *believe*.

But what is the magic cure?

The magic cure is a complex algorithm of applied ideals, time-honored rituals, and genuine forgiveness. The magic cure starts with understanding and accepting four specific facts:

- There is only one magic cure. Stop seeking more.

- Your views of life skew your life. Open your eyes and see how your true SELF affects you, the windows to your soul, and the people you know.

- Ritualistic changes work when your rituals are focused on your self-determined purpose. Start by first determining your purpose. Then... you can start doing things on purpose. Start today.

- You are not perfect, and neither is anyone else. Unless you can honestly say you have never hurt, harmed, or hindered anyone, you owe it to your SELF to forgive everybody for everything.

In reality, you are the magic cure.

Acknowledgements

Thank you for reading this book.

In my well-travelled life, there are so many people who have taught me the profound nature and beauty of the Absolute Truth.

Ironically, I have learned from an equal number of "good" and "bad" people. I seem to have learned the most from the least of us, and I have learned the least from the preeminent hierarchy of people in powerful positions of authority.

But I have mostly learned from the Great Spirit that led you to this book. I have learned at the time and rate at which I was supposed to learn. And, undoubtedly, I will learn so much more as I continue my path along life's spectacular journey.

I am often forgetful of, but always thankful for the vast depth and expanse of knowledge of which I was blessed before I read my first book, heard my first word, or saw my first teacher.

Through this very book, I acknowledge the most important person in the world: you.

I acknowledge the fact that we *believe* different things; yet we *live* by the same requirements.

I acknowledge that, while you may have learned a few nuggets of knowledge within this short book, I am no better, no stronger, and no higher than you.

I thank you for reading this book.

About the Author

John H. Clark III is an idealistic realist who has achieved *The Ideal* life by writing and sharing the Truths contained in this book. *The Ideal* is real.

Formerly educated at the University of Memphis and The Naval Postgraduate School, John has shared insights from his international travels and lifelong journey of leadership, while assisting organizations and individuals achieve success outside of the traditional thoughts and limitations of conventional methodologies. *The Ideal* is real.

As Founding President of *The Positive Information Exchange,* John launched an altruistic platform for creating synergistic relationships that transcend simple ideas, simple rhetoric, and divisive conjecture. *The Positive Information Exchange* is a pathway to an idealistic-but-real place. By incorporating Truth and ideals, everyone... including students, families, organizations, and individuals... can go far beyond current mindsets, risky relationships, learned restrictions, and confusing misinterpretations. *The Ideal* is real.

According to John, "By featuring Truth and ideals, we create the seemingly impossible from the great realm of the possible. By focusing on possibilities, we create the probable from the prescribed and proposed. By prescribing Truth and ideals, the seemingly impossible becomes a simple roadmap to a perfectly achievable dream." *The Ideal* is real.

To schedule John for an event, please visit

www.JohnClarkiii.com

John H. Clark, III
Author
Optimistic Realist

Founder and President
The Positive Information Exchange

www.ThePositiveInformationExchange.com

www.ingramcontent.com/pod-product-compliance
Lightning Source LLC
Chambersburg PA
CBHW070348090426
42733CB00009B/1339